BE ENCOURAGED!!!

250 DAYS OF MOTIVATION AND ENCOURAGEMENT

My goal, every day that I am here on this earth, is to inspire and encourage others!

Make it your daily mission as well!

By Michael Arterberry

Short-term thinkers plant gardens...
Long-term thinkers plant trees.
Eternity minded thinkers plant
themselves in the souls of others!

~ Michael Arterberry

I've had the honor of knowing Mike Arterberry for more than 40 years. We first met in elementary school where he was among the tallest and most athletic of second graders - charismatic beyond his years and above all else, incredibly kind. Kids of all ages identified with Mike the way they do with superheroes. They watched in awe as he modeled good sportsmanship, leadership, and did whatever he could to include those who were typically left out or kept on the fringe socially. All these years later, it is no surprise that Mike continues to inspire others. To watch him in action with others, is to see a real-life superhero who gains your trust, speaks your language, and demonstrates that your past need not define your future. To me, Mike is proof-positive that people come into our lives for a reason so, in the year that we both turn 50, I consider it a privilege to remain personally connected to the man he's become. I look forward to seeing how Mike's remarkable journey unfolds and continue to marvel at the impact he makes on the world. I guarantee you'll be motivated by his spirit, and taken by his intuitive nature. You will, most certainly, Be Encouraged!

-Leanne Tormey, EdD

This book undoubtedly contains nuggets of wisdom that have the power and potential to change your life. How do I know that? Cause I know the man who wrote it. As his Pastor, I have watched Mike grow and become a person who has dedicated his life to impacting the lives of this generation with the wisdom he has learned and applied to his life. He is a man of character, faith and integrity and I know the pearls of wisdom he shares have the power to bring supernatural peace to your life!

Pastor Frank Santora – Lead Pastor Faith Church NYC, ATL, CT

www.faithchurch.cc

I have had the pleasure of coaching Mike Arterberry since his days as a young football player at Albert Leonard Jr. High School in New Rochelle, NY and then again in both High School and at Iona College.

Michael was a gifted and talented athlete who came to us from humble beginnings. Originally known for his physical toughness as a player, we quickly learned that he had great mental toughness as well dealing with his own issues and injuries. As a coach, I always preached Team and Family first. As I look at Michael's life over the years, I see a Man, a Christian, who embraces his humble beginnings, and who has a "Game Plan" on how to move forward in a positive manner, always treating people with respect.

Michael has overcome obstacles in his life and he has done so with great motivation and drive. He understands life's challenges, understands that Team Work and Hard Work do pay off. He accentuates the "Positives" and shares that it is okay that you have struggles in your life, or that you have been knocked down. There is no quit in Michael as he shows us that how we respond to our problems is what defines us. He knows what it is like be disciplined, to face life's challenges in a positive way and to be successful.

He understands and believes that _"Winner's Turn Obstacles into Stepping Stones"_.

Harold Crocker

Director of Athletics

Ramapo College of New Jersey

My life is dedicated to moving people from an uneasy time in their lives to a place of peace. I can't change their circumstances, but I can help change their perspective.

I help them understand that it's not about the destination, but the battles won along the way. I encourage them to hold on and understand that bad doesn't look bad when there is good in it.

People will follow you if you inspire them. I work hard to inspire, lead, encourage, and celebrate the people that come into my life.

BE ENCOURAGED!!!

Don't allow your history to dictate your destiny.

"His fingerprints are all over it!" ~ Pastor Frank Santora

"I am a warrior ready to fight. And yes, I have lost people and things along the way. But I realize what I lost, no longer matters." ~ Angela M.

I dedicate this book of motivation to Angela M., always positive, always a warrior…she fought the good fight!

The power of making a decision. 23

Withhold criticism and be patient. 24

Show life today how good it can be. 25

Stuck 26

How Good You Have It. 27

Perhaps the most dangerous relationship is the one most
difficult to spot..28

Live Life as It Comes. 29

Listen to Your Heart...30

I Knew You When. 31

Doubt kills. 32

Life is not an experience, it's a journey...................................33

We have to learn to not only praise GOD in our good times.
....34

Where are you?..35

Think of your life as a Potter and Clay...................................36

Stuck in the past..37

When people are under pressure, they look for someone to
blame. 38

The enemy of vision is sight...39

I may not be where I want to be, but I'm glad I'm not where I
used to be..40

What do you do when you feel overwhelmed with life?......41

Be the person who brings positive energy into a room.........42

Have you ever thrown your entire self at anything?..............43

Big people think like eagles and little people think like
chickens. 44

Life brings us many assaults. 45

Battles 46

"Father Hunger"..47

God is with you in your storm..48

Journey 49

God thinks in Seeds; we think in Trees. 50

What purpose do you serve? 51

Life has a tendency to hand you something you didn't expect. 52

There is power in passion...53

Perception is everything and there is a danger in a flawed perception. 54

Safety raft 55

Going through the process is very important................56

Winners congregate together. 57

The process gives you the foundation. 58

You have to stretch out your mind.................................59

I'm not afraid of death as long as I live first. 60

Creative people break rules..61

The people who rejected you do so because they see you as a problem..62

There is a danger in low expectations. 63

Being committed and having controversy is not easy..........64

Destiny has a rhythm. 65

Miracles begin with recognition of what you already have.66

There is a purity in simplicity. 67

There is a purpose in your problem. 68

What almost happened to me. 69

It's not so important what we say to God......................70

People of the world who have much are sometimes wasteful. 71

Your past is a point of reference. 72

God is the master of little things...............................73

There are moments in life that will try the human soul. 74

Where is your cross?..75

You will always go where you are thinking. 76

Power without strategy is dangerous.......................77

Just because you may be in your wilderness doesn't mean that you are lost. 78

The feeling of transition makes us very uncomfortable.........79

When God shines the light on you, it will produce heat. 80

You are under attack because of your influence. 81

There is a difference between provision and promise. 82

When you plant a seed it's destiny concealed. 83

What do you fight for other than a paycheck? 84

The secret to elevation. 85

The greatest test is how you handle power. 86

Bitter people blame others for their problems. 87

Your personality whispers secrets of what your purpose is. ..88

Life is a University; it will teach us many lessons. 89

Are you shipwrecked on the road to your destiny? 90

When we look at our lives in small pieces, we don't see the strategy of the good and bad................................91

Focus is too important to be compromised...........................92

Do you live with a feeling that you have been short changed? 93

You will get so much out of it that you would do it for free..94

We often fall in love with new beginnings.............................95

Poverty can be generational because it has a culture. 96

Get your life into focus. 97

Do you have a destiny? 98

Exceptional and ordinary will always have conflicts. 99

Can God trust you with trouble or are you here just for the ride? 100

It's all about perception. 101

Some people go through the actions of commitment but are never really committed to anything. 102

It takes courage to just let things go. 103

Have you ever had life just punch you in the face?...........104

It's a dangerous thing to want to be like other people.......105

What takes people's appetite for life?...................................106

Don't drown in shallow water. 107

Freedom begins in the mind..108

Stop being in love with where you came from. 109

Some of us have come from rags to riches. 110

My agony makes my ecstasy..111

Don't get pushed into a position where you don't fit. 112

The voices in your head are fighting to gain control of how you see your situation..113

There is a specific plan and purpose for your life.................114

The miracle is not in what you lost. 115

Friends and opportunists look exactly the same. 116

The strength of the crop controls the net worth of the holder. 117

You cannot be great without the ultimate sacrifice. 118

You have to finish whatever you start.................................119

The harvest of a sacrificial life. 120

When dealing with the unexpected, resist the quick fix. 121

Without a vision, people will perish...........................122

Our strength is in our struggle. 123

God has a plan for your life......................................124

I refuse to settle for what is not the best for me...................125

You have to rise above the challenges in your life.............126

If you don't have hope, faith doesn't have a job. 127

You cannot be a champion until you survive a breaking point...128

Where there is no investment there is no return. 129

We live life with the guilt of not being enough.....................130

Intelligence is different than education. 131

Our success is made out of the ingredients of our struggles. 132

When passive and aggressive faith collide, God gets bigger in your life. 133

All life gives you are moments in time.......................134

"I don't know " is not commonly used. 135

I found God in the middle of my chaos. 136

Your life is a series of sowing and reaping.......................137

The death of radicalism. 138

Forgetting the things that are behind me..........................139

A goal is just a goal until you write it on paper...................140

We are Sheltered by the Sheppard. 141

Nothing in your life just happens without a purpose. 142

You don't have time to live in one emotion.........................143

Progress is not hindered by your environment.....................144

People use things to cover up where they really are in life.
....145

I finally got my head back...146

Do you have the focus to be successful? 147

So many people want promotion without going through the
process. 148

Silk worms turning into butterflies. 149

Symbols are important because they remind us of where we
came from. 150

When people can walk away from you, let them walk.......151

Why do you think or feel God falls asleep in the middle of our
storms?...152

If we want to reach our destiny, we have to remove some
barriers. 153

Rise above it and don't quit. 154

The importance of the right outlook. 155

Failure is associated with the feeling of almost making it...156

God is more concerned about His purpose rather than your
comfort..157

You will smile again, it's only a matter of time.....................158

The giraffe and the turtle occupy the same space............159

What feeds you? 160

What you see on the outside is a reflection of what is going
on in the inside..161

You can find God in the middle of chaos............................162

Don't squander your gift, use it to gain. 163

I am what I do. 164

Surviving on broken pieces..165

Once you say something out loud you can't take it back. 166

Did you ever think you were doing something good, and it turned bad?...167

It's one thing to plant a seed and watch it grow, and another thing to build something from the ground up. 168

The beauty of in between. 169

Faith does not mean that God does your work for you......170

Sometimes we have to sneak up on success.......................171

As I try to figure out this thing called life. 172

There is a point for your pain. 173

Don't get angry about your mode of transportation through your journey. 174

Don't judge what is in you by what you see around you. ..175

Just because a person is silent, doesn't mean that they are ok..176

How bad do you want it?...177

The power is in the valleys of your life. 178

Sometimes it is easier to not want anything than to want something and not get it. 179

The power is not in the gift...180

You would be surprised what people will pay to fix up the outside. 181

Do I run or do I fight? 182

Creative people are people who break the rules...............183

You don't need to be empowered if you are not going anywhere. 184

At peace with yourself; one with yourself. 185

We are running out of time. 186

Every teacher is forever a student...187

True leadership breaks rules..188

Are you appreciated? 189

What did God hope for when he made you? 190

Honor this day...191

We have to recognize God in our storms.............................192

Anytime God wants to do something special in your life, he does not give you many details...193

Pay attention to what is probable......................................194

Do you sometimes find yourself in the wilderness? 195

It is no accident that you came into this world head first...196

Love fades when conditions change. 197

We all have battles. 198

Do you have the urge to just quit? 199

Are you looking at life correctly?...200

Living with criticism...201

Do you feel like you are stuck in between places? 202

The enemy knew who you were going to be before you got here. 203

People want to incarcerate you on how they understand you to be. 204

There is nothing more powerful than a changed mind. 205

Sometimes, somebody else's success exacerbates your own frustration..206

Your life is a direct reflection of the voices you listen to......207

God is a lover and giving is for lover's only............................208

Are you putting a demand on life, or is life putting a demand on you?..209

A proper outlook on life is necessary to change our lives...210

Look back over your life..211

Living with uncertainty is very hard. 212

There is discipline in doing. 213

If we stay aware, we will realize that God illuminates our steps. 214

If you look at this world through the eyes of logic, you will go crazy. 215

Our desires have to be purged in the fire of prayer. 216

There are some miracles that require human involvement to get them started. 217

Don't take the presence of the storm to indicate the absence of God. 218

You have to get out of your comfort zone. 219

It's hard to be big when little has you. 220

You attract the energy you exude. 221

Be honest with life, be honest with others and, most of all be honest with yourself. 222

Exceptionalism is often incubated in the womb of adversity. 223

Peace is yours to choose regardless of what else may be going on in your life. 224

Life is about a fight and you have to keep fighting. 225

There is a difference between worldly peace and spiritual peace. 226

We have to learn to trust God when He says no. 227

The real of today is in the living of it. 228

Real trouble is a humbling experience. 229

You are a living letter for all to read. 230

Things generally don't work themselves out, you have to work them out yourself. 231

There is a difference between being buried and being planted. 232

You can bring good things out of bad places. 233

We all have our own personal nest. 234

Don't let where you start define where you are going........235

Life has a tendency to teach us lessons. 236

Don't let the negative words spoken over your life determine who you become. 237

There is no happiness in poverty and no happiness in the palace. 238

It's not the success that shows who you really are. 239

Faithful are the words of a friend. 240

The mind is a powerful, complicated, sophisticated machine. 241

Do you have the instinct to increase in your life? 242

Stop running. 243

How can something be in the will of God and still go wrong? 244

Information means nothing without revelation. 245

The potholes in your life don't come with announcements or road signs. 246

Light always casts a shadow. 247

The perfect gift is from above. 248

What is the destiny that God has for you? 249

Life is a series of being drawn out. 250

When you have a strategy that aligns with your purpose you don't need much to make it work. 251

The principle of sowing and reaping is not magic. 252

Fear is powerful, and yet fragile. 253

Experiences versus our instincts is what keeps us in our cage. 254

Your mind is your power. 255

We must have the instinct to shift gears. 256

The Core of the Matter 257

Don't be a dreamer or a wannabe. 258

Listen, your instincts may be telling you that this could be a destiny moment. 259

God's answers don't always look like what we have in mind. 260

Failure is associated with the feeling that you are almost there 261

The world works in systems of cycles. 262

We all have survived something and have had the urge to quit. 263

Sometimes we are in a wilderness where nothing grows. ..264

We are running out of time. 265

If you want to win the battle of life, you have to stay on track. 266

Where is your faith? 267

A lesson in humility. 268

You have to work with the skin that you were born with. ...269

Surviving is not enough. 270

God gives you trials to prepare you for what is coming next. 271

Exceptional and ordinary always have a conflict. 272

THE POWER OF MAKING A DECISION.

If bad decisions get you into trouble then good decisions will get you out. There is a danger in not making a decision at all. Some people are where they are because they have made no decision at all. You've had opposition and opportunities but you are afraid to make decisions because of the risks. When you are passive with the decisions over your life, you take the chance of missing your turn. Some people are stuck where they are because they choose to be stuck.

BE ENCOURAGED!!!

"Thank you, I needed to hear this today." ~ Laura B.

"I am encouraged." ~ Leopold G.

WITHHOLD CRITICISM AND BE PATIENT.

If you are not careful, you will quickly judge the actions of others. Remain open minded, quiet, and loving because we don't know all of the circumstances. Open your heart and listen to others' stories.

BE ENCOURAGED!!!

With your attitude and actions, prove to the world that life is worth living. Be reminded that even the smallest light can break through the darkest darkness, enabling other light to shine through.

BE ENCOURAGED!!!

STUCK

If it seems that you're stuck where you are, no matter what you do, then you're almost certainly trying too hard. Stop trying and start allowing. Life is beautiful to a degree that goes far beyond anything you can possibly imagine. Stop trying to imagine that beauty and start allowing yourself to experience it.

BE ENCOURAGED!!!

HOW GOOD YOU HAVE IT.

Remind yourself today how good you have it, then allow yourself to make it better. Treasure what you are thankful for and be thankful for what you treasure.

BE ENCOURAGED!!!

PERHAPS THE MOST DANGEROUS RELATIONSHIP IS THE ONE MOST DIFFICULT TO SPOT.

They are seemingly kind, apparently loving, whispering flattering words and sweet promises. They are the proverbial wolves in sheeps' clothing. They are false friends and malicious manipulators who lead you to believe they are acting in your best interest. In fact, they are not thinking of you at all. We must remain vigilant for these predators who smile and whisper soothing words, hypnotizing us with deceptive charm while all along trying to exploit our kindness.

BE ENCOURAGED!!!

LIVE LIFE AS IT COMES.

Though you have pains and problems and challenges, you also have the good fortune of being able to have life, as it is, from where you are, with what you have. Breathe deeply, gently, and peacefully. Feel the miracle of your own existence. Live life as it comes.

BE ENCOURAGED!!!

LISTEN TO YOUR HEART.

Whether you're up or you're down, whether you're confident or unsure, listen to your heart. Your heart knows why you are here. Your heart knows about possibilities that your mind has not yet considered.

BE ENCOURAGED!!!

I KNEW YOU WHEN.

You may be being held back by an " I knew you when" crew. They keep you stuck in a stage of your life that is past and gone. These people define you on the basis of who you *were*, not who you have become, and certainly not who you can someday be. They want you to linger with them on memory lane. They rob you of the momentum you need to soar. They will not permit you to embrace the future. You need to move beyond the "good old days". The past is over and cannot be rewritten. It can only be played out over and over again. It is time to write the rest of your story.

BE ENCOURAGED!!!

DOUBT KILLS.

Don't let someone who gave up on *their* dreams talk you out of yours. Doubt kills more dreams than failure ever will.

BE ENCOURAGED!!!

LIFE IS NOT AN EXPERIENCE, IT'S A JOURNEY.

Life is a winding road with twists and turns, laughter and pain. You don't get to stay on top of the mountain or in the valley because life is a journey. You sometimes learn things on the mountain as well as in the valley. A conflict or challenge you may be going through has not happened to destroy you. What you are going through right now has presented itself so that you can make adjustments. You are on a journey from speculation to revelation.

BE ENCOURAGED!!!

WE HAVE TO LEARN TO NOT ONLY PRAISE GOD IN OUR GOOD TIMES.

We must also praise Him in our dark times. God shows Himself strong in our dark times. God lives in our hard places and He is the bridge between where we are and where we see ourselves. Many times, we get caught up in our circumstances and think God is invisible, but the reality is that He is always present. Quiet your spirit and you will feel Him.

BE ENCOURAGED!!!

It all starts with you! There is something deep inside, moving and driving you. It burns inside of you, wanting to get out. Assume responsibility for where you are. Don't hide in the bushes of excuses. Take charge of your situation because success is made out of failure.

BE ENCOURAGED!!!

THINK OF YOUR LIFE AS A POTTER AND CLAY.

God is the Potter; we are the Clay. We must understand that God is the master teacher and that we are a work in progress. God spins us on the Potter's wheel shaping us to who He wants us to be. Sometimes it feels like we are spinning out of control, but we are not because God is in control. We spin speedily and time is the measure of its effectiveness. Never forget that God can take something that is broken, hold it in His hands and make it whole, just like the Potter's Clay.

BE ENCOURAGED!!!

STUCK IN THE PAST.

Clinging to and nourishing vindictive hurts and grudges will eat your soul, consume your happiness, and rob your creativity. Similar to blame, this junk keeps you stuck in the past. You often won't know what you have, let alone what you need in your life, until you clear the mental and emotional room to experience the here and now.

BE ENCOURAGED!!!

WHEN PEOPLE ARE UNDER PRESSURE, THEY LOOK FOR SOMEONE TO BLAME.

The spirit of blame comes out of frustration. Some conversations are pointless because they don't bring change. I can't be around people that say 'never'. These people are cursing those around them, their conversations curse your life. Don't be like old salt that has lost its flavor. Be a new person, a new creation. Until you are liberated, your mind will be in turmoil.

BE ENCOURAGED!!!

"One of the hardest lessons in life is letting go. Whether it's guilt, anger, love, loss or betrayal. Change is never easy. We fight to hold on and we fight to let go." ~ unknown

THE ENEMY OF VISION IS SIGHT.

Sight is the function of the eyes, and vision is the function of the heart. Never trust your eyes over your vision. Vision shows you what could be, and sight shows you what is. Your vision is more than your present reality. Vision is the source of confidence. Cut the umbilical cord of yesterday so you can exist today.

BE ENCOURAGED!!!

I MAY NOT BE WHERE I WANT TO BE, BUT I'M GLAD I'M NOT WHERE I USED TO BE.

You cannot judge your life by where you are now, especially if it is a place you don't want to be. You have to be careful not to make permanent decisions for a temporary problem. Stop putting so much energy into a place in life that you are going to evidently move from.

BE ENCOURAGED!!!

WHAT DO YOU DO WHEN YOU FEEL OVERWHELMED WITH LIFE?

You pray and your prayer is overruled by God. We must trust God when He says no because the tougher the day, the greater the strength He gives us. Seasoned Saints are overjoyed in tribulation and little saints are overjoyed when they come out of trials. You will win if you don't quit. God's Grace Is Sufficient!

BE ENCOURAGED!!!

BE THE PERSON WHO BRINGS POSITIVE ENERGY INTO A ROOM.

Be the person who reminds everyone else how good it can be to be alive. Joy costs you nothing to give, and it can mean so much to everyone it touches. Today, give joy, live joy, and experience life at its best.

BE ENCOURAGED!!!

HAVE YOU EVER THROWN YOUR ENTIRE SELF AT ANYTHING?

Success is about being committed. Don't get stuck in a place of limited thinking. You have not had your greatest day yet. It is somewhere inside of you. You are a miracle waiting for a place to happen. What is hiding in you that you haven't seen? We are running out of time. This is your time, be determined to live it.

BE ENCOURAGED!!!

BIG PEOPLE THINK LIKE EAGLES AND LITTLE PEOPLE THINK LIKE CHICKENS.

Fly above your circumstances and do not get overwhelmed by your struggles. God cannot give you your blessings for the future when your hands are full of your past.

BE ENCOURAGED!!!

LIFE BRINGS US MANY ASSAULTS.

When these assaults come, we must hold our posture and remember that God is our security system. You can't speak peace outwardly if you don't have peace inwardly. Anybody can dance in sunny weather. God wants us to praise Him in stormy weather. Secret prayers reap public answers. God's greatest gifts come wrapped up in problems and chaos. His gift often worries us before it blesses us. Don't allow fear to rob you of God's gift for your life.

BE ENCOURAGED!!!

45 | P a g e

BATTLES

In a short period of time you can go through a lot of situations that make you want to quit and give up. Look at these situations as battles because some of us get beaten in the battle and some of us get better in the battle. Everything God promises will meet us in our greatest place of pain.

BE ENCOURAGED!!!

"FATHER HUNGER".

A smile from a Dad is like 20 kisses from a mother! There is a king in every boy and a boy in every king. When someone shows you the king, it makes you control the boy in you. We are losing our boys because we are not listening for their silent screams.

BE ENCOURAGED!!!

GOD IS WITH YOU IN YOUR STORM.

Don't ask Him to preserve the temporary. People and things are brought into our lives to get us from A to B. Many of us get caught up in holding onto the temporary. Don't let life overwhelm you; we can survive it with broken pieces. Don't drown in shallow water, just stand up.

BE ENCOURAGED!!!

It is not your destination in life that is most important. It's what you learn on your journey.

BE ENCOURAGED!!!

GOD THINKS IN SEEDS; WE THINK IN TREES.

The Tree is in the Seed!!! God puts Great things in Little things. For every Struggle in your life there is a Strategy!!!

You don't have to be popular to be powerful!!!

We have peaks and valleys in life and because of my faith I am able to survive the valleys. I try not to get preoccupied with where I'm at, but instead always try looking forward to where I'm going.

BE ENCOURAGED!!!

What do people get when they get you? What do people lose when they lose you? Life should be about serving a purpose. We must serve a higher power and be more selfless rather than selfish.

BE ENCOURAGED!!!

LIFE HAS A TENDENCY TO HAND YOU SOMETHING YOU DIDN'T EXPECT.

It will demand that you pick up the pace. There is danger in low expectations. We have to run after our destiny because as we run for what is in front of us, we escape what's behind us.

BE ENCOURAGED!!!

No passion, frigid, cold, indifferent, average people never get much in life because they don't want anything bad enough. They are not willing to take a risk, but there is power in passion. Passionate people apply continual pressure and wear it down. They are relentless and never stop fighting until they get what they want. They refuse to live in neutral.

What are you?

BE ENCOURAGED!!!

PERCEPTION IS EVERYTHING AND THERE IS A DANGER IN A FLAWED PERCEPTION.

What looks like a road block is just redirection. What feels like an obstacle is just an opportunity. Don't miss opportunities in your life because you don't perceive your value.

BE ENCOURAGED!!!

SAFETY RAFT

Do I stay in the safe familiar raft of my past experiences and cling to my past perceptions? Even in the face of new opportunities, do I have the courage to release my grip on the raft of past ideas? Letting go allows you to dive head first into a pool of a bigger stream of consciousness.

BE ENCOURAGED!!!

GOING THROUGH THE PROCESS IS VERY IMPORTANT.

Where you are now is a test, but not your destination. Start where the opportunity is because you are in transition. The process is in preparation for the minimal things which lead to mighty things.

BE ENCOURAGED!!!

WINNERS CONGREGATE TOGETHER.

There is a mentality that goes along with winning. There is also a pathology to losing when you are limited by your current conditions. There is a difference between process and purpose. The process will bring you to your purpose and a stable place. Once you reach this stable place, you can't live in fear that you are going to lose it again.

BE ENCOURAGED!!!

THE PROCESS GIVES YOU THE FOUNDATION.

There are no shortcuts to excellence. In this microwave generation, we have lost all sense of slow preparation. The underground work must be done before the above ground work is exposed.

BE ENCOURAGED!!!

YOU HAVE TO STRETCH OUT YOUR MIND.

If you don't, you will not be able to change your thinking, functioning, and perception. The body at rest stays at rest. The first time you stretch, it will hurt but you have to stretch over the pain. The same with life; your crises and challenges put you in a position to stretch.

BE ENCOURAGED!!!

I'M NOT AFRAID OF DEATH AS LONG AS I LIVE FIRST.

What I'm more afraid of is to exist without living. Most people live and die in a wilderness of uncertainty. Your fear is your enemy. You are afraid of the wrong thing. You should be more afraid of not accomplishing what you were created for than you are of the difficulties and challenges along the way.

BE ENCOURAGED!!!

CREATIVE PEOPLE BREAK RULES.

Breaking the rules of routine deliberately removes the barriers in your life and changes the game. You must color outside of the lines. How you have defined yourself stops you from exploring yourself. Be creative, shatter your reality and walk right into your dreams.

BE ENCOURAGED!!!

THE PEOPLE WHO REJECTED YOU DO SO BECAUSE THEY SEE YOU AS A PROBLEM.

Just because others may see you as a problem doesn't mean you can't be an answer. Growing up, we first learned to add then we learned Algebra. Addition shows you the problem, problems looking for the answer. Algebra is an answer looking for a problem. The reason you haven't been successful is because you think you are a problem looking for an answer. In fact, you are an answer looking for a problem.

BE ENCOURAGED!!!

THERE IS A DANGER IN LOW EXPECTATIONS.

Success is never an accident. You have to run after your destiny. When you run after your destiny, you distance yourself from your history.

BE ENCOURAGED!!!

BEING COMMITTED AND HAVING CONTROVERSY IS NOT EASY.

Being committed and disappointed are not easy. Being committed without recognition is not easy. Being committed and not being appreciated is not easy. Surround yourself with people who are fit for the fight and the work, and not just for the fun.

BE ENCOURAGED!!!

DESTINY HAS A RHYTHM.

There is a rhythm I must have around me to keep me motivated. Don't change my rhythm. You change my rhythm, you kill my creativity. The strength of your life is in the rhythm. Have you been living your life without a rhythm? Everything great has a rhythm. Life is controlled by a rhythm. You are off beat or delayed because you don't have the discipline to get into rhythm.

Get into the rhythm of champions.

BE ENCOURAGED!!!

MIRACLES BEGIN WITH RECOGNITION OF WHAT YOU ALREADY HAVE.

If you don't recognize what you have, it can't multiply. God will always use that which wasn't counted to produce the miracle. The best miracles take time and can't be driven by hunger, need, or necessity. The blessing is in the breaking. The more it is broken, the more it multiples. I thank God for all the times He walked with me through my broken times. Let's recognize what we already have and open our hearts to what God wants to do for us.

BE ENCOURAGED!!!

THERE IS A PURITY IN SIMPLICITY.

We have to be able to operate in the middle of chaos.
Everything doesn't have to be right to be functional.

BE ENCOURAGED!!!

THERE IS A PURPOSE IN YOUR PROBLEM.

There is a purpose in your pain. There is a purpose in your adversity. There is a strategy in your misfortune. You must have an expectation that things will change or you will lose your miracle.

BE ENCOURAGED!!!

You would be surprised what misfortune passed over me; what should have killed me; what should have taken me out; what almost happened to me; what happened to my friends but didn't happen to me; what happened to my family member but didn't happen to me; what happened in my neighborhood but didn't happen to me. I should have been a statistic, a case study, lost my mind. When it came to get me, there was a shift. Things passed over me for a purpose.

What has passed over you?

BE ENCOURAGED!!!

IT'S NOT SO IMPORTANT WHAT WE SAY TO GOD.

What is most important is what God says to us. Sometimes there is so much noise around us we cannot hear His voice. We must be able to hear Him because He is our navigation system. The way the navigation works in your car is how God works in your life. He wants to speak to you to help you through this season of your life. Anytime God wants you to do something important for Him, He doesn't give you details. God will not only use the destination, but also the journey to train you to hear His voice. He may not be big on details, but He is committed to the process. If you have the courage to step into the unknown, God has the power to do the impossible.

BE ENCOURAGED!!!

" I love how your life has developed my friend. You have passion and to me that is most important." ~ John F.

PEOPLE OF THE WORLD WHO HAVE MUCH
ARE SOMETIMES WASTEFUL.

I want to tell you that God is moved by hunger. Some people have the whole loaf of bread. You have only a crumb and you are working that thing. Remember that miracles are in the leftovers so never step over them.

BE ENCOURAGED!!!

YOUR PAST IS A POINT OF REFERENCE.

Some people find it hard to get into their future because their past is chasing them. There is no life in what you lost. If you can think of yourself differently, you will live differently.

BE ENCOURAGED!!!

GOD IS THE MASTER OF LITTLE THINGS.

God gives you an acorn when you ask for an oak tree because He knows the oak tree is in the acorn. Don't despise small beginnings. Small things will test your character but will have major ramifications. Show me a door that is closed; there is a key to open it. Don't cry over what you lost; be thankful for what you have left.

BE ENCOURAGED!!!

THERE ARE MOMENTS IN LIFE THAT WILL TRY THE HUMAN SOUL.

We have to be careful because discouragement can sneak in secretly. Discouragement is so bold that it will hide behind a smile. We have to take proper steps to overcome our situation. Steps imply process. You can't get to the destination just because you want it. Don't make a permanent decision on a temporary circumstance.

BE ENCOURAGED!!!

What kills your pride, challenges your deepest fears, or that you endure for a greater cause? Where is your faithfulness and consistency? Until you have a cross you have no right to ask for a crown.

Real value is determined by sacrifice.

BE ENCOURAGED!!!

YOU WILL ALWAYS GO WHERE YOU ARE THINKING.

Transformation starts from the inside out and the renewing of your mind. If you want a true transformation, change what you are thinking and it will change where you are going. You have to get ready for where you are going and not where you were.

BE ENCOURAGED!!!

Power without strategy is explosive and lethal. Power channeled correctly with strategy makes it functional, great energy, and life changing. So many people are dressed up and going nowhere because they are so focused on the external rather than the internal.

BE ENCOURAGED!!!

JUST BECAUSE YOU MAY BE IN YOUR WILDERNESS DOESN'T MEAN THAT YOU ARE LOST.

Your current circumstance doesn't prove who you are. You are what you are hungry for, that's why you crave it. You wouldn't crave love if you weren't a lover. You wouldn't crave wisdom if you weren't wise. You wouldn't crave giving if you weren't a giver. The only reason you want excellence is because you are excellent.

Your present situation doesn't predict your future.

BE ENCOURAGED!!!

THE FEELING OF TRANSITION MAKES US VERY UNCOMFORTABLE.

Anytime something changes, we freak out. We get anxious worrying about something that didn't even happen yet. We all have patterns, cycles, behaviors, and routines that need to be broken. Break your normal because your normal is your prison.

You cannot fit in and standout.

BE ENCOURAGED!!!

WHEN GOD SHINES THE LIGHT ON YOU, IT WILL PRODUCE HEAT.

You can't have light if you can't handle more heat. Each battle brings you to another level. Promotion is boobie trapped so the imposter can't get to it. It costs to be a winner.

BE ENCOURAGED!!!

YOU ARE UNDER ATTACK BECAUSE OF YOUR INFLUENCE.

You are not always alerted about changes in your life that affect, disrupt, and take you out of your comfort zone. The test and challenge are a compliment. You are great, mighty, and strong. Your direction comes from your rejection. Your greatness is incubated through your frustration. The more frustrating the environment, the more fruitful the individual.

BE ENCOURAGED!!!

THERE IS A DIFFERENCE BETWEEN PROVISION AND PROMISE.

Provision is how God sustains us as we are waiting for the promise. When you get to the promise, provision will be in it. The promise makes you smile in the rain and laugh at the pain. When the provision stops, be strong because it's a sign that you are there. Every setback is a set up for a comeback. Provision is not promise. So many fall in love with what is transitional and miss what is permanent. Provision is the bridge to promise.

BE ENCOURAGED!!!

WHEN YOU PLANT A SEED IT'S DESTINY CONCEALED.

To have increase is destiny revealed. Watering is the transition point between what is concealed and what is revealed. Without watering, the destiny will remain in the ground where it was planted. You plant the seed so it can be watered and come back greater than it was.

BE ENCOURAGED!!!

WHAT DO YOU FIGHT FOR OTHER THAN A PAYCHECK?

Do you associate with a cause besides yourself? Do all roads lead back to you? Every great person, generals, presidents, civil rights leaders, people worth studying were people who found a cause greater than themselves.

BE ENCOURAGED!!!

THE SECRET TO ELEVATION.

When your relationship brings you to a level you're not supposed to be in, " Shut your mouth ". You are only there to catch a glimpse of where you are going. Stop trying to be important on a level you haven't arrived at yet. Stop trying to make a contribution beyond your intellect. There are levels that you must humble yourself to. The climate changes as you climb the ladder of success.

BE ENCOURAGED!!!

THE GREATEST TEST IS HOW YOU HANDLE POWER.

Powerless people have to get power from somewhere else to even fight. You can't turn a wrong into a right without power. What do you do when you have the edge? Is it all about *you* or is it about *us* and *we*?

BE ENCOURAGED!!!

BITTER PEOPLE BLAME OTHERS FOR THEIR PROBLEMS.

Bitterness is when the issues on the outside have contaminated the person on the inside. Being bitter affects your life; allowing your past to bleed into your present and pollute your future. Because life puts you on pause doesn't mean it has stopped you all together. When you are bitter, you cannot trust your own judgment.

Take responsibility for your actions and move on with your life.

BE ENCOURAGED!!!

YOUR PERSONALITY WHISPERS SECRETS OF WHAT YOUR PURPOSE IS.

Look at your story because there you will find clues to the secret of what lives deep in your soul, of what you were meant to be. You are bigger than what you have been used for so far in your life.

BE ENCOURAGED!!!

LIFE IS A UNIVERSITY; IT WILL TEACH US MANY LESSONS.

Do you know what it is to deal with a fight on the inside while dealing with a fight on the outside? It's easier to stop a fight on the outside than to stop the fight on the inside. Life situations will draw things out of you that you didn't even know were in you. Frustration will always express itself because you can only hide it for the moment. Frustration is a sign of investment. We get frustrated because investment creates expectations.

BE ENCOURAGED!!!

ARE YOU SHIPWRECKED ON THE ROAD TO YOUR DESTINY?

What do you believe? What you believe has to do with the philosophy you live by. Your vision, purpose, and goals are what defines who you are. The predicament you are currently in does not define your destiny. You know how to say the right things, but what's most important is doing the right thing.

BE ENCOURAGED!!!

WHEN WE LOOK AT OUR LIVES IN SMALL PIECES, WE DON'T SEE THE STRATEGY OF THE GOOD AND BAD.

Good and bad are working together to accomplish a particular purpose. When you have a strategy that aligns with the purpose of your life, it doesn't take much to make it happen. Stop getting up in the morning to see what is going to happen, or let other people control what's going to happen. As you seek your purpose, the clue is in the passion.

What are you passionate about?

BE ENCOURAGED!!!

FOCUS IS TOO IMPORTANT TO BE COMPROMISED.

You have to focus on what is important. Refuse to be distracted by other people's problems. Do not put energy into things that are not profitable. You have to be committed to being progressive, and not repetitive.

BE ENCOURAGED!!!

DO YOU LIVE WITH A FEELING THAT YOU HAVE BEEN SHORT CHANGED?

We all have an area of our lives where there is inequity; the sad memories of missed or lost opportunities. Well, now is the time you are going to step into a new dimension. Your life is about to be revolutionized. A major opportunity is coming to you. Remember that out of small places will come big things.

BE ENCOURAGED!!!

YOU WILL GET SO MUCH OUT OF IT THAT YOU WOULD DO IT FOR FREE.

Once you find your purpose, it satisfies you completely. You might make money from it but the money is a byproduct of finding your purpose. Finding your purpose is not a race to the biggest seat. The seat doesn't have to be a big thing to be an important thing. What matters is that it's important to you.

BE ENCOURAGED!!!

WE OFTEN FALL IN LOVE WITH NEW BEGINNINGS.

Everything that starts one way doesn't always end that way. As soon as you master the class, you get moved to the next level. You have outgrown the capacity of your current position. Growth is always disruptive; it will always create structure and strategy. Something is going to happen that will make everything you've been through make sense. Make your pain pay you, make it profitable.

BE ENCOURAGED!!!

POVERTY CAN BE GENERATIONAL BECAUSE IT HAS A CULTURE.

Poverty is not about not having money. It's about a mindset and mentality. Once you get into that poverty mentality, money can't bring you out. Your mind will rob you of the opportunity your money gives you. Miracles are made out of need. You never know how much you got in you until you are challenged by more than what you see.

The power is in what you have left.

BE ENCOURAGED!!!

You have to be more progressive and refuse to be repetitive. You have to make every step count. Forget about the things that are behind you and press towards the things in front of you. Stop putting your energy into things that are not profitable.

BE ENCOURAGED!!!

DO YOU HAVE A DESTINY?

You are not here on this earth by mistake. You are here because you have a destiny to fulfill. When you know you have a destiny, there is a nagging, annoying feeling in your gut. It just won't leave you alone. Don't let anything get in your way of your destiny. Don't let people define you by what they see when they meet you because you are on your way to your destiny. There is more to you than what people can see. There is a sleeping giant inside of you that is waiting to be awakened.

BE ENCOURAGED!!!

EXCEPTIONAL AND ORDINARY WILL ALWAYS HAVE CONFLICTS.

My question to you is will you be ordinary, fit in with the pack, run with the wolves, or will you step out to be exceptional? When you are exceptional, you can't hang out with ordinary people. They don't speak the same language. Life is all about enjoying the great moments of your life. Be exceptional. a trend setter, a rule breaker.

Say to yourself, " I am exceptional ".

BE ENCOURAGED!!!

CAN GOD TRUST YOU WITH TROUBLE OR ARE YOU HERE JUST FOR THE RIDE?

Show up for the party not the problem; the blessing and not the burden. We have to learn to do it when it's good and not good; when it's right and not right; when we feel like it and when we don't. You have to ride it out. Look at your situation and say 'God chose me for this assignment because He knew that a lesser man or woman would have caved from the struggle'. What's pulling you down from the mountain top? Keep climbing and reach the destination that was meant for you today.

BE ENCOURAGED!!!

IT'S ALL ABOUT PERCEPTION.

You may be going through some real challenging times in your life. Nothing you seem to do is able to straighten it out. At what point did you stop expecting change? I want you to look back to when you almost gave up. Your time has come, you are about to come out. If you kill it in your head, you kill it in your life.

BE ENCOURAGED!!!

SOME PEOPLE GO THROUGH THE ACTIONS OF COMMITMENT BUT ARE NEVER REALLY COMMITTED TO ANYTHING.

You cannot have a relationship without reciprocity. You cannot get into a relationship to get but never give. Ask yourself, do you give as good as you get? I would hate to live and die and never know if I committed myself to anything. Some people have never thrown their entire self into anything. Without reciprocity, no relationship will reach its apex because you are not fully invested. Always casual and never committed, your life is a false advertisement. When you get me, you get help. I will always add something to you.

What do people get when they get you?

BE ENCOURAGED!!!

IT TAKES COURAGE TO JUST LET THINGS GO.

It is difficult to let things go that hurt you, wounded you, broke you, and caused you pain. It takes faith to believe that what is in front of you is greater than what's behind you. If you don't learn how to forgive you cannot live, thrive, or move forward. You will always suffer. If it lives in your head, it lives in your life. If you are distracted with what used to be or could be, you miss what is.

BE ENCOURAGED!!!

HAVE YOU EVER HAD LIFE JUST PUNCH YOU IN THE FACE?

Life is not over. Stop sitting on the sidelines nursing your wounds and get back into the game. It's time to be revived and live again. There is nothing more dangerous than a person on the comeback because you have nothing to lose. There is nowhere to go but up.

BE ENCOURAGED!!!

IT'S A DANGEROUS THING TO WANT TO BE LIKE OTHER PEOPLE.

Anytime you wish to be someone else, you lose your uniqueness and distinctions. The power is in truly being yourself. As long as you feel life has cheated you, you will never enjoy where you are, always grieving what you think you should have had. You have to get tired of feeling sorry for yourself and just live.

BE ENCOURAGED!!!

Pain takes so much attention and focus that all sensation of pleasure and fulfillment is sacrificed when people hurt. Has something taken away your appetite? Someone died last night, gasping for air, trying to make it to this morning. You woke up complaining and doing nothing with your life. We need to start living life and maximizing every minute of every day.

No one is promised tomorrow.

BE ENCOURAGED!!!

DON'T DROWN IN SHALLOW WATER.

It seems to be a ridiculous notion that you could drown in shallow water, especially when you have survived the deep. It's hard to believe that you can drown in something you could normally handle. The toughest times of life are not in the struggle. In the beginning of the struggle you are fresh, vibrant and ready. The truth, is when you are closest to the shore, you are the most vulnerable. Don't preserve the temporary. Success is not defined by the temporary. It's defined by working with what you have left.

BE ENCOURAGED!!!

FREEDOM BEGINS IN THE MIND.

Some of us are free physically but not mentally. When you free your mind, you can change your circumstances. What's going on in your head can be more real than what is going on in your life. The images you have seen have the world to do with who you are now.

BE ENCOURAGED!!!

STOP BEING IN LOVE WITH WHERE YOU CAME FROM.

Start falling in love with where you want to be. Escape the prison of your past that holds you back from seeing the light of your future. Let it go and free yourself to run in the wild of your destiny and purpose.

BE ENCOURAGED!!!

SOME OF US HAVE COME FROM RAGS TO RICHES.

We have to learn from what life has provided for us which is considered our rags. Our rags are a voucher; a symbol of what we are going to do with what we have left. We are going to have good days and bad days. When you have good days, take them and seal them in a box. On the bad days, take a peak inside that box to remind yourself.

BE ENCOURAGED!!!

MY AGONY MAKES MY ECSTASY.

It's a painful thing to be a visionary. A visionary sees what shall be and wakes up to deal with what is. It's my sickness that makes my healing. It's my poverty that illuminates my prosperity and makes me appreciate where I am now.

BE ENCOURAGED!!!

DON'T GET PUSHED INTO A POSITION WHERE YOU DON'T FIT.

Some people spend 20 to 30 years being pushed into a position where they don't fit. They could have been used, but they were abused. Abuse is the just the abnormal use of who you really are. This happens because people need you to be like something you are not. We can get caught up trying to shape ourselves to fit someone else's needs. You cannot be who you were and who you need to be at same time.

BE ENCOURAGED!!!

THE VOICES IN YOUR HEAD ARE FIGHTING TO GAIN CONTROL OF HOW YOU SEE YOUR SITUATION.

If you are not careful, your mind will faint over the fatigue of the struggle. Ask yourself, are you complaining about things that others dream about? Just walk with your struggle until you walk out of it. We must learn to say no to the lesser so we have room to say YES to the greater.

BE ENCOURAGED!!!

THERE IS A SPECIFIC PLAN AND PURPOSE FOR YOUR LIFE.

As you look back over your life, you will see patterns. You will see patterns in your weaknesses, dilemmas, decisions, and friends. Do you have goals for your life or are you just living? If you don't have goals, then you don't have any direction.

In the game of life, nothing just happens.

BE ENCOURAGED!!!

THE MIRACLE IS NOT IN WHAT YOU LOST.

The miracle is not in what you previously consumed. Your best days are not your yesterdays. Your miracle is what you have left. The blessing is in the breaking. The greatest blessings come in the hardest breaks of your life.

BE ENCOURAGED!!!

FRIENDS AND OPPORTUNISTS LOOK EXACTLY THE SAME.

They both smile in your face, but the opportunist will run away from you when things get tough. Friends will stand by you in times of adversity. You don't get to choose your family but you do get to choose your friends. Don't connect with people from where you came; connect with people for where you are going. I'm careful not to waste my high octane love on low octane engines. My love is too rich to be planted in poor soil.

BE ENCOURAGED!!!

THE STRENGTH OF THE CROP CONTROLS THE NET WORTH OF THE HOLDER.

The perpetual cycle of sowing and reaping is in working, never taking time off, even in your reaping season. Success doesn't always look like how you've imagined it. You don't recognize your season of success because you focus more on your situation. This just distracts you from maximizing your harvest.

BE ENCOURAGED!!!

YOU CANNOT BE GREAT WITHOUT THE ULTIMATE SACRIFICE.

We live our lives wanting to be great, but not willing to make the ultimate sacrifice to be great. The ultimate sacrifice is in serving others. Stop being a taker, only doing things that excite and feed you. You have to submit to the mission of something bigger than you. There is a dance between sensual and spiritual. Sensual is centered around self-gratification, and spiritual is denying 'I' for the greater cause.

Without purpose, life has no meaning.

BE ENCOURAGED!!!

YOU HAVE TO FINISH WHATEVER YOU START.

When you don't finish what you start, you have to live with the infection of not finishing. This infection will infiltrate all parts of your life. Push yourself when no one is looking. Embrace who you are. Know that anything is possible.

There is no substitute for hard work.

BE ENCOURAGED!!!

THE HARVEST OF A SACRIFICIAL LIFE.

Foundational truth is what causes a spiritual awakening. You must have balance between your faith and the real world. You have grace and truth, power and principles, anointing and intelligence. You don't have to sacrifice one for the other. God is not reasoned; He is revealed. Whenever there is an object in light, there is a shadow. Be the beauty, light, and glow that steps into a room.

BE ENCOURAGED!!!

WHEN DEALING WITH THE UNEXPECTED, RESIST THE QUICK FIX.

Quick fixes have a tendency to increase the damage. Sometimes doing the right thing at the wrong time can destroy everything. Stop, look and listen to your spirit before you make a permanent decision to a temporary circumstance.

BE ENCOURAGED!!!

"Thank you. Appropriate for me right now." ~ Maria B.

WITHOUT A VISION, PEOPLE WILL PERISH.

You may not be able to touch it, but if you can see it with patience, you can wait for it. Where you are now will not last because there is something out there that you want.

BE ENCOURAGED!!!

OUR STRENGTH IS IN OUR STRUGGLE.

Every conqueror has had complications and struggles in their lives. If you wait for the complications to leave, you will never be a conqueror. The fact that I'm a conqueror is through my complications. When God opens up a door, circumstances don't matter. Go into this week as a conqueror and get your fight back.

BE ENCOURAGED!!!

GOD HAS A PLAN FOR YOUR LIFE.

Just ask him to show you where you fit. You will never know where you *do* fit until you find out where you *don't* fit. Anyone God has used in a mighty way was rejected by other people. You are broken in all the right places. He broke you so that He can increase you.

BE ENCOURAGED!!!

I REFUSE TO SETTLE FOR WHAT IS NOT THE BEST FOR ME.

People who settle have a maybe in their answers. The maybe is how they tranquilize their hope because they don't want to deal with the pain of not attaining their vision. As you progress towards your vision, cut away anything that is not essential to where you are going or isn't productive. When you change your game, change your name...rebrand yourself. You cannot be who you were and who you are at the same time. Your goal is to be great, but you don't have to say it. What you do should be an announcement to the world that you are great.

BE ENCOURAGED!!!

YOU HAVE TO RISE ABOVE THE CHALLENGES IN YOUR LIFE.

Get ready for what God is about to do next. You have to fight and keep the faith. Do I have any fighters out there? You will lose a lot of things along the way, but you have to keep fighting and keep believing.

BE ENCOURAGED!!!

"I am a warrior ready to fight. And yes, I have lost people and things along the way. But I realize what I lost, no longer matters." ~ Angela M.

IF YOU DON'T HAVE HOPE, FAITH DOESN'T HAVE A JOB.

Hope is an expected end. Hope has nothing to do with a process, but everything to do with destination. Don't become satisfied with something that should only encourage you that you are in the right place. How do you want to be remembered? I will continue to strive to leave a sign that I was here. I will leave a legacy that my children's children will know that when I passed through the world, I left my footprint.

BE ENCOURAGED!!!

YOU CANNOT BE A CHAMPION UNTIL YOU SURVIVE A BREAKING POINT.

It doesn't matter where you start; it's where you finish. The difference between the start and the finish is how you answer the breaking point. The greater the pressure the more we tend to isolate ourselves which can terminate our dreams. Dreams cannot be accomplished on your own. I realized the importance of partnerships. Partnerships don't have to be parallel to be productive as long as they cross paths at the intersection of purpose. Profit is tied to purpose, and profit without purpose is a "me" mentality and does not work. God can only promote you to the level of your tolerance to pain. Your strength will make you tough enough to get there, and your weakness will make you humble enough to be grateful once you arrive.

BE ENCOURAGED!!!

WHERE THERE IS NO INVESTMENT THERE IS NO RETURN.

Your greatest fear should be to finally get your moment and not be ready. Preparation is never time wasted. You have to get ready for something that hasn't even happened yet. Work towards what you feel on the inside but can't see on the outside. You have to be ready so that when a door opens, you can step through. The difference between a dream and a goal is a deadline.

Invest in your dream and make it a goal because opportunity has a deadline.

BE ENCOURAGED!!!

"This is probably one of the best ones of the year. Your posts help me through each day. Reminding me of safe, healthy ways to continue my life." ~ Jayme L.

WE LIVE LIFE WITH THE GUILT OF NOT BEING ENOUGH.

Everybody has a story, and in that story, we wrestle with many things. You will be surprised about the stuff you worry about that just doesn't matter. Just a word of advice, if it doesn't affect your purpose and destiny, it just doesn't matter. If you are not careful, you will live a life of worry, then look back and realize that none of the worry was necessary. The unfortunate thing is that you don't get that time back. When your mind goes to that place, fight it, enjoy the moment and live a more powerful and peaceful life.

BE ENCOURAGED!!!

INTELLIGENCE IS DIFFERENT THAN EDUCATION.

I've seen educated people who were not intelligent, and intelligent people who were not educated. Our lives are a direct reflection of the voices we listen to. Anytime someone has your ear, they influence you and your thoughts. My purpose in life is to give others insight into their lives, to find the mystery and purpose. Your purpose is the compass to your life. Once you find your purpose, there is peace, happiness, and fulfillment added to your life.

BE ENCOURAGED!!!

OUR SUCCESS IS MADE OUT OF THE INGREDIENTS OF OUR STRUGGLES.

We need to have closure with past experiences to move on with our lives. We cannot allow our history to control our destiny. As much as you may not like it, nothing in your life just happened. There is a reason why you went through what you did. Your life experiences had purpose. Your destiny is tied to everything you have been through.

BE ENCOURAGED!!!

WHEN PASSIVE AND AGGRESSIVE FAITH COLLIDE, GOD GETS BIGGER IN YOUR LIFE.

Your problems become smaller. When you get the grace to get out of your situation, you have to move quickly. Stop laying around in your mess. When God's glory shows up in your life, He's going to give you back all that you lost. He will give you double for your trouble.

BE ENCOURAGED!!!

ALL LIFE GIVES YOU ARE MOMENTS IN TIME.

All you miss about a person are the moments. You don't have weeks and years, you have moments. You have to create your own moments, but you can't stay there. After moments you have to move on to a mission. The mission is where you make sacrifices to help others.

What are you willing to sacrifice where there is no benefit to you?

BE ENCOURAGED!!!

"Did you write this for me? ~ Anne-Marie W.

"I DON'T KNOW " IS NOT COMMONLY USED.

People don't want to look bad in front of others. If you live life long enough, it will humble you to admit things you do not know. If you are always the teacher, you are going to run out of things to teach. When a teacher is forever a student, the class is always exciting. We have to be able to transition roles or we will run out of gas.

BE ENCOURAGED!!!

I FOUND GOD IN THE MIDDLE OF MY CHAOS.

In finding Him, I realized that His Blessings come in His timing. The chaos was Him grooming me for my Blessing. My season is not only coming, but it's here. God has been preparing me for where I'm going. God can only Bless what you are doing. God Blesses doers not thinkers, dreamers, or wishers. Never underestimate the effort of doing. We are so shocked by the trauma of the chaos that we run from the process. You think you are waiting on God, but God is waiting on you. God says He will Bless it if you create it.

This is my year. I have big plans and I'm going to work this thing. I'm going to work in the field of my dreams, hopes, and desires. I will not stop until God Blesses it.

Watch out world here I come!!!

BE ENCOURAGED!!!

YOUR LIFE IS A SERIES OF SOWING AND REAPING.

You sow certain things, so that you have a right to expect certain things in return. There is one problem and that is we all have conflicts in our gardens. It seems like every time you are about to be the most productive, here comes a conflict. Don't be discouraged by the chaos and challenges in your life. This is your season because conflict comes when you are about to move to the next level.

BE ENCOURAGED!!!

THE DEATH OF RADICALISM.

Too many people are striving to be peculiar rather than revolutionary. Radical people make a difference. When you are radical you must be willing to stand out, be criticized, and talked about. Radicalism is not rewarded initially; it's rewarded in hindsight. What are you called to change? Everything you do, everything you touch is a result of somebody's idea.

BE ENCOURAGED!!!

FORGETTING THE THINGS THAT ARE BEHIND ME.

Reaching for the things in front of me. I'm going to learn to enjoy the present moment. Until you are open to the moments of in between, you will miss the greatest moments of your life. What could be wrong with your life now is that you are not there. When life called roll call for today, you were not present. You were dealing with yesterday and striving for tomorrow.

BE ENCOURAGED!!!

A GOAL IS JUST A GOAL UNTIL YOU WRITE IT ON PAPER.

Then it becomes a vision. But before you think of your vision, you must have an imagination. You have to imagine yourself out of your current situation. Know that before greatness is accomplished, your comfort zone needs to be disturbed. There is a certain mentality that's associated with winners; perseverance and repositioning yourself. Reinvent yourself when necessary and don't let anything get in your way.

So, what is your vision?

BE ENCOURAGED!!!

Have you gone through a situation that should have destroyed you? I want you to look back and think about all the things that could have happened, should have happened, and almost did happen. You can't understand how you got through it. God covers us like a mother bird covers her eggs. In order to get through this, you have to go through Him. No matter what you are going through right now, no matter how painful it is, know that you are not alone.

BE ENCOURAGED!!!

NOTHING IN YOUR LIFE JUST HAPPENS WITHOUT A PURPOSE.

Your situation is part of the plan for your life. We were custom made to be able to go through our trials and challenges. It's like getting a suit tailored. The tailor measures all of your bodily dimensions so that when the suit is cut, it fits you perfectly. Your situation is tailor made to fit your personality and demeanor. Just remember to come through without an attitude, but with a mindset of gratitude.

Where you started will turn into where you are going.

BE ENCOURAGED!!!

YOU DON'T HAVE TIME TO LIVE IN ONE EMOTION.

Life is always yin and yang, up and down, good and bad, all at the same time. You have to learn how to be happy, sad, careful, and excited in the game of life. The problem is not where you want to go, but what are you willing to leave behind to get there.

BE ENCOURAGED!!!

"Leaving it all behind." ~ Ketti G.

PROGRESS IS NOT HINDERED BY YOUR ENVIRONMENT.

Geese are not defined by their environment. They walk on land, swim in water, and fly in the air. Stop defining yourself by who you used to be. Make changes, get a fresh perspective and don't let your history control your destiny.

BE ENCOURAGED!!!

PEOPLE USE THINGS TO COVER UP WHERE THEY REALLY ARE IN LIFE.

I was telling my children this morning about the hard life I lived, filled with suffering and struggles. But I'm not angry. These things put the fight, determination, and drive deep inside me. I had to be tested with obscurity before I could be trusted with notoriety. Your strength is not proven in your accomplishments and successes. Your strength is tested with your tenacity when all hell is breaking loose.

BE ENCOURAGED!!!

I FINALLY GOT MY HEAD BACK.

I was living my life from a heart place rather than from a head place. I was governed by my emotions, having my heart fight in a head battle. I was living a headless life because I couldn't separate how I felt from what I know. Our feelings will never equal our dreams. I was a kingdom without a king because I was too busy managing my feelings and the feelings of those around me. Progress only happens when you get your head right. The heart cannot save the brain, but the brain can save the heart. With every blessing there is a battle. The greater the blessing the greater the battle.

BE ENCOURAGED!!!

DO YOU HAVE THE FOCUS TO BE SUCCESSFUL?

Most people live a life without order and structure. Bringing things into order in your life is a sign of maturity. Your response to pressure and stress should be order and structure. You must have the structure that is consistent with where you are going and not where you have been.

BE ENCOURAGED!!!

SO MANY PEOPLE WANT PROMOTION WITHOUT GOING THROUGH THE PROCESS.

You will find greatness once you master smallness. People are busy trying to progress when they haven't mastered where they are. If you don't see your full potential in the rehearsal, you won't see it in the recital. Be patient with the process and not enthralled with the promise. Your future is kin to your past. You are the acorn of the oak tree. Your destiny will bring the tree out of the nut.

Stop being in love with tomorrow and neglecting today.

BE ENCOURAGED!!!

My wish for all of you is that all the good things inside of you will manifest themselves and come out of you. We need transformative thinking because there are Kings and Queens inside of us all. I want you to become a new you. We are all in the process of transforming to a higher, better expression of ourselves. Never lose the desire to evolve and the possibility to change.

BE ENCOURAGED!!!

SYMBOLS ARE IMPORTANT BECAUSE THEY REMIND US OF WHERE WE CAME FROM.

Moments frozen in time help you remember what you made it through. Symbols are personal and mean something to each individual. Symbols are priceless. You may be dealing with an issue, challenge, or crisis. Use your personal symbol to give you the strength to fight through. Learn how to use what life handed you rather than complaining. Some people wouldn't believe where you have come from.

BE ENCOURAGED!!!

WHEN PEOPLE CAN WALK AWAY FROM YOU, LET THEM WALK.

Your destiny is never connected to anyone who left. There is a secret fraternity for people who have endured pain in their lives. You feel for other people because you can relate to their pain. Always remember that nothing ever just happens.

God has a plan for your life.

BE ENCOURAGED!!!

WHY DO YOU THINK OR FEEL GOD FALLS ASLEEP IN THE MIDDLE OF OUR STORMS?

He knows we can handle it. What you need to get through the storm is in you, not around you. We spend too much time focusing on what's around us rather than what's in us. You have to take time to get to know who you are. How can you expect others to know who you are if you don't know who you are? Chaos, trouble, denial, rejection, and hard times taught me what was inside of me. I didn't know I could encourage myself. I've panicked and called people for wisdom that was weaker than the wisdom I had myself. In your body, you have world consciousness. In your spirit, you have God consciousness. In your soul, you have self-consciousness. Divine expectations…if you don't expect anything you won't receive anything.

BE ENCOURAGED!!!

IF WE WANT TO REACH OUR DESTINY, WE HAVE TO REMOVE SOME BARRIERS.

The way we speak, understand, and think is a system that we create to manage life. Some of us are mature on the outside, but immature on the inside. Our system is the system we used as a child. Are you reacting to stimulation like a child? Are you understanding like a child? Are you being victimized by you? We have outgrown our current system and need to upgrade. Your old system is blocking you from opportunities. When you change your system and way of understanding, it gives you the expected outcome. Stop fighting to hold onto a system that is blocking you from your best life.

BE ENCOURAGED!!!

It's not about winning, it's about finishing the course. You can quit and still be physically present. Just because you are physically present, doesn't mean you are spiritually, emotionally, mentally present. Defy the urge to quit. So many quit and it was only one more step to cross the finish line. You cannot win if you don't fight. You will win if you don't quit because the best is yet to come.

BE ENCOURAGED!!!

THE IMPORTANCE OF THE RIGHT OUTLOOK.

I can tell how healthy you are inwardly by your outlook on life. Your outlook is a reflection of what is going on inside you. The power is in what you see. Life sends us obstacles, trials, and struggles to blur our vision. You can't have the right outcome if you don't have the right outlook. Take back control of your thoughts and become the driver of your car, not the passenger.

BE ENCOURAGED!!!

FAILURE IS ASSOCIATED WITH THE FEELING OF ALMOST MAKING IT.

When we are threatened and intimidated, we run back into our comfort zone. There are some places we used to fit, but we don't fit anymore. We talk about the God that opens doors, not considering the God that closes doors too. God is not a way, He IS the way! He has the key to your next opportunity.

BE ENCOURAGED!!!

GOD IS MORE CONCERNED ABOUT HIS PURPOSE RATHER THAN YOUR COMFORT.

Sometimes He will make you uncomfortable so He can bless you later. God's strength is made perfect in your weakness.

BE ENCOURAGED!!!

YOU WILL SMILE AGAIN, IT'S ONLY A MATTER OF TIME.

People who sow in tears will reap in joy. What makes the mountains high are how low the valleys are. You have the power within you to make it right. The process to help you understand your pain has been slow and progressive. Something good is going to come from you.

BE ENCOURAGED!!!

THE GIRAFFE AND THE TURTLE OCCUPY THE SAME SPACE.

The turtle eats at the level of its vision. The giraffe eats at the level of its vision. One eats grass while the other eats from the TOPS of trees. Whenever turtles comment on the giraffe's vision, you cannot trust it because it's a reflection of their world view. Many of us pay too much attention to the comments from the turtles around us.

What are you, a turtle or a giraffe?

BE ENCOURAGED!!!

WHAT FEEDS YOU?

You have to strive to be able to adapt to diverse situations. The more flexible you are, the larger your life can be. Being narrow minded will limit you to the possibility of opportunities. Where do you get your information? You are no better than what you eat. Whatever you eat impacts the outcome of your life. Stop throwing simple solutions at complicated problems.

BE ENCOURAGED!!!

WHAT YOU SEE ON THE OUTSIDE IS A REFLECTION OF WHAT IS GOING ON IN THE INSIDE.

There are so many grown men and women walking around with little boy and little girl issues. The fight on the outside will force you to deal with the fight on the inside. The test of greatness is to survive frustration. Adversity is always connected to opportunities. As for your haters, learn about who you are from them. Their hatred of you is a tutorial on your significance in this world. The simple fact that someone finds you important enough to talk about is your validation. Often your prophecy is in the mouth of your enemies.

BE ENCOURAGED!!!

"This is fantastic." ~ Angela M.

YOU CAN FIND GOD IN THE MIDDLE OF CHAOS.

All the chaos, long standing problems and troubles are just a set up. It's a set up because when God delivers you, there will be no doubt in His authenticity. What we go through in our lives are merely opportunities for God to show up.

BE ENCOURAGED!!!

DON'T SQUANDER YOUR GIFT, USE IT TO GAIN.

Gifts that you are born with are the hardest to see because they are considered normal to you. Remember, something you don't recognize, you can't utilize. You will suffer from low self-esteem trying to find your worth when it was inside you all the time. Continue to be creative because if you are predictable you are replaceable. It's all about what you do with what you have.

BE ENCOURAGED!!!

I AM WHAT I DO.

Performance based understanding of yourself. You try to earn your way through life. Possession based understanding of yourself. I am what I have. Validation that comes from stuff. You will sell your soul for a bowl of soup. Popularity based understanding of yourself. If enough people like me, I am. Your value comes from others (Instagram, Facebook) I'm popular because I have 1000 followers. It's hard to bring things from your thought life into action. You have to know, be, and just do it.

BE ENCOURAGED!!!

Life is a journey. Sometimes we deal with gentle storms that move us to where we need to go, but there are times when we are in full blown hurricanes. Stop trying to manage what you can't but stay on the ship. Build yourself up; spend some quiet time; build up your spirituality with good spiritual food because the last part of the journey is always the hardest. The entire ship may not make it but grab what is left. We must learn to make it on broken pieces. You don't have what you used to have, but if you hold onto what is left, you are going to come out of it alright.

BE ENCOURAGED!!!

ONCE YOU SAY SOMETHING OUT LOUD YOU CAN'T TAKE IT BACK.

Sometimes our mouths get us into a lot of trouble. When you have said something wrong, be mature and own it. Sometimes we have to be the bigger person. It's not always about winning the battle.

BE ENCOURAGED!!!

"Thank you." ~ Amy M.

DID YOU EVER THINK YOU WERE DOING SOMETHING GOOD, AND IT TURNED BAD?

After you have messed up, do you feel as if there is this dark cloud over your life? Make the best of a bad situation. What do you do when you have tried and failed and you want to give up? Do it again!!! This is not how your story is supposed to end. There is more for you than what *you* have put in place to fill the void. God is going to give you something new to replace the old. Look for divine replacement.

BE ENCOURAGED!!!

"...to never be in that place again!" ~ Karen C.

"Thanks bro for positive words of encouragement. I stand in agreement today with You on this. Sometimes or probably most times these denials or setbacks are blessings and if God chooses the doors will open in the right season. Thank you for sharing hope." ~ Vincent B.

IT'S ONE THING TO PLANT A SEED AND WATCH IT GROW, AND ANOTHER THING TO BUILD SOMETHING FROM THE GROUND UP.

God speaks to us in Agricultural and Architectural terms. People don't like building much in our microwave, self-serve, instant gratification society. You have to build first by design; you need to have a vision and a plan. You also need to have a strong foundation. Things can look good on the outside, but what does your foundation look like? If you build from the ground up, you know what you have, and can withstand storms, and trials. This is not about a house; this is about your life. Building implies that there is going to be a lot of work. Are you up for the task?

BE ENCOURAGED!!!

THE BEAUTY OF IN BETWEEN.

We are so afraid to be vulnerable. We have become masters of disguises. The energy we spend to protect ourselves from others. Stop living your life like you are Dead. What you use to protect yourself and insulate yourself has now incarcerated you. You are missing the pain, but also missing the joy. If you can't be vulnerable, you can't grow. There is nothing in your history controlling your destiny. Until you open yourself to the here and now, you will miss some of the greatest moments of your life. Maybe your life would be better if you were there sometimes. You are looking to when and missing now. So, by anticipating tomorrow, you cheapen today.

BE ENCOURAGED!!!

FAITH DOES NOT MEAN THAT GOD DOES YOUR WORK FOR YOU.

Are you building a life that God can bless? If you have real faith, you have to be willing to look like a fool for a little while. Are you willing to be a fool for God? Some people have too much pride to be willing to be a fool. Everyone around you is looking at what is, you are looking at what's next. Put all your efforts into your future and not your past. Your past can be a mess, but your future can be amazing.

BE ENCOURAGED!!!

SOMETIMES WE HAVE TO SNEAK UP ON SUCCESS.

Some of us talk so much about success that we delay our success. Our mouths are too big for where we are trying to go. Because we announce everything, we further jeopardize what we want to happen. Remember some of our greatest moments are hidden in our mess. Remember that the wisdom you seek from others on the outside, you actually have somewhere deep inside you. I like to call it "Hidden Treasure ".

BE ENCOURAGED!!!

AS I TRY TO FIGURE OUT THIS THING CALLED LIFE.

I realize that pain has purpose. It's not about what I lost, it's about what I'm about to gain. The only way I can motivate others to be survivors is to have gone through or go through things myself. Test, distress, delivery, trusting promise…the cycles of life.

BE ENCOURAGED!!!

THERE IS A POINT FOR YOUR PAIN.

When storms and challenges come into your life, they can stop you from being able to think and reason. They can stop you from being who you really are. You have to know that the storm is a strategic attack on your life. They are designed to prevent you from pressing towards your destiny and impacting the world. It's about your influence. You have to change your perspective and outlook.

BE ENCOURAGED!!!

DON'T GET ANGRY ABOUT YOUR MODE OF TRANSPORTATION THROUGH YOUR JOURNEY.

Any storm you have been through was not meant to kill you but was meant to push you. The journey will sometimes feel like it's working against the promise. It's not the destination that is important, it's the things you learn along the way. The journey is where you get your wisdom, fight, tenacity, determination, and survival skills. You will not show up to your destination until you have gone through your journey. Remember we have to shake that dirt.

BE ENCOURAGED!!!

"In this I believe!" ~ Gayle S.

DON'T JUDGE WHAT IS IN YOU BY WHAT YOU SEE AROUND YOU.

You have to have hope. Hope is the star and faith is the supporting actor. If you don't have hope, faith doesn't have a job. Hope is an expected end, not a specific process. Don't be satisfied by something that should only encourage you that you are going in the right direction. Refuse to live and die and not leave something on the earth that's a sign that you were here.

BE ENCOURAGED!!!

JUST BECAUSE A PERSON IS SILENT, DOESN'T MEAN THAT THEY ARE OK.

They may have mastered the art of camouflage, painting a smile on their face. Going through their expected duties, but that doesn't mean that they are ok. What we need to do is speak out when things are not right. The fight is in your mind because your mind is where promises are planted. You are in a fight over the spirit of your mind.

BE ENCOURAGED!!!

Surviving is not enough. So many times, we make the best out of a bad situation, or bring down our expectations to match our reality. We build systems around something we lost faith in that we could change. We begin to define ourselves by a dysfunction. Your desires direct your destiny and if you don't want anything, you're not going to get anything. You can't be casual about it; you have to go get it.

Exceptional desires get exceptional results.

BE ENCOURAGED!!!

THE POWER IS IN THE VALLEYS OF YOUR LIFE.

Highlights are made in the dips of your life. It's how you survived the valleys that make you powerful. You survived the valleys through the memories of good times. What is hiding in you that you have not yet seen? You have what it takes. All of your struggles have made you fit for the fight.

BE ENCOURAGED!!!

SOMETIMES IT IS EASIER TO NOT WANT ANYTHING THAN TO WANT SOMETHING AND NOT GET IT.

It costs you something to have expectations. You have to be tough, tenacious, and resilient to wait for your breakthrough. You have to say to yourself, "I may not have it, but I want it". You have to refuse to think that where you came from is a definition of where you are going. Your history is not your destiny. It costs you something to change your life and survive your past. I want to share with you that your breakthrough is here; this is *your* year. My only advice is to have the strength to be able to make it happen and be ready for it. This is your time and season.

BE ENCOURAGED!!!

"It's good to have goals and seek to achieve things, but what I'm finding is contentment and a grateful heart for all God has already blessed us with goes a long way—but mainly for God alone! and no matter what does or doesn't happen we can enjoy the peace from God." ~ Vincent B.

THE POWER IS NOT IN THE GIFT.

The power is in the love. The ultimate gift is the love of God. His love turns our misery into our ministry. He turns your pain into your passion. The ultimate gift leads to the ultimate experience (Life). If you want to give the ultimate gift, give someone the love that God has given to us. It's not just what you desire and what you want to receive. It's about what you are willing to give. Give and it will be given to you.

BE ENCOURAGED!!!

YOU WOULD BE SURPRISED WHAT PEOPLE WILL PAY TO FIX UP THE OUTSIDE.

Make up, implants, and injections…We must build ourselves from the inside out. We have to put more emphasis on the foundation than the building. We have to start right to end right. We should want to produce good fruit, but if there is no love in the seed, there will be no love in the fruit. The fruit you produce must smell of love because it started in a place of love; love for ourselves and the love for others.

BE ENCOURAGED!!!

Instincts are most important in pivotal parts of your life. Do I walk away or do I stand? Instincts are important when you near a turn in your life. When opportunity passes by, potentially powerful things can happen. All the pain of unrealized passion tells you this is the moment. Anytime you break up with how you saw yourself, it's a painful conversation, but necessary. You cannot be who you were and who you are at the same time.

BE ENCOURAGED!!!

CREATIVE PEOPLE ARE PEOPLE WHO BREAK THE RULES.

Don't be incarcerated by the rules around you and live life with limits. If you want to do something great, you have to be willing to color outside the lines. You cannot be a trendsetter if you are traceable. Believe the dream more than the reality, shatter the reality and step into the dream.

BE ENCOURAGED!!!

"Yes, I still believe in this, that's what I follow in my life. To be different you have to think or do things another way and that improves your creative workflow, instead of following the original way that others think that will bring success to their career or dream..." ~ Asha B.

YOU DON'T NEED TO BE EMPOWERED IF YOU ARE NOT GOING ANYWHERE.

You don't need to put gas in a parked car. Stop being impressed with who you are. Stop being selfish and start thinking of others. We've become a narcissistic society in which everything is about *you*. Many have not been trained to serve others. So many are occupied with the benefits of life, but are not doing the job. Let's practice paying it forward and change the world one act of kindness at a time.

BE ENCOURAGED!!!

AT PEACE WITH YOURSELF; ONE WITH YOURSELF.

A oneness being in harmony. You feel you are not good at anything, but you are perfect for your purpose. The difference between a C note and a C cord is a C cord allows someone to sing in harmony with the key of C, but do it in the context of the individual's range. Harmony means you can be different as long as you fit in your range.

BE ENCOURAGED!!!

WE ARE RUNNING OUT OF TIME.

What are you going to do with the time you have left? You must reposition yourself so you don't miss the best time of your life. Change the way you think and function. You have to be tough and use the difficult times in your life to break the barriers of limitations. You are a miracle waiting to happen.

This is your moment; be determined to live it.

BE ENCOURAGED!!!

"I AM a miracle. Period." ~ Angela M.

EVERY TEACHER IS FOREVER A STUDENT.

You cannot teach further than you learn. The path of God is delivered in glimpses not detail. When you are chosen, you will be forever pulled apart. When God gives you glimpses, He sets you apart. Because of the uniqueness of your path, you cannot be common with your associations. Living life can sometimes be a lonely business if you are really going to follow God. He is going to call you apart. Faith is not proven on top of the mountain, it is proven in the valley. The faith proven in the valley makes you eligible for the mountain top. Everyone who has gotten an upward call wrestles with downward cravings. I don't despise the struggles. We often underestimate what it takes to be successful. Following God will take you where the air is thin and the climate is cold. I would rather have thin air and the cold climate than to have full air and comfortable climate in the valley.

BE ENCOURAGED!!!

TRUE LEADERSHIP BREAKS RULES.

You cannot be a leader and always comply. A leader is prepared to go where no one has gone before and do what they said you couldn't do. If you live within the fences, you are not a leader. If you color within the lines, you are not a leader. Leaders do what somebody said cannot be done. Being a leader can be a lonely place.

BE ENCOURAGED!!!

Anytime people take you for granted, you cannot perform at the level you could if they appreciate who you are. Their attitude robs you of your power because you are the most potent when you are the most appreciated.

BE ENCOURAGED!!!

WHAT DID GOD HOPE FOR WHEN HE MADE YOU?

Could you be doing things that just don't matter? What gifts
are inside of you? God hid your inheritance in your trash.
There is treasure in your trash.

BE ENCOURAGED!!!

HONOR THIS DAY.

Honor the possibilities in this day, honor the love and the beauty in this day. Look around at all you have. In this moment, make it, in your own way, something truly great. See the wonder and the beauty all around you and let yourself truly love who you are and where you are in the moment.

BE ENCOURAGED!!!

WE HAVE TO RECOGNIZE GOD IN OUR STORMS.

God uses our storms to train us. New challenges are a sign of progress. Be careful not to allow your past to shape how you see the present. Operate from a position of strength and not strain. Don't be afraid to encounter God in a different form than when He usually comes to you.

BE ENCOURAGED!!!

ANYTIME GOD WANTS TO DO SOMETHING SPECIAL IN YOUR LIFE, HE DOES NOT GIVE YOU MANY DETAILS.

He uses the journey not the destination to train you to hear His voice. You have to be able to hear His voice to recalibrate the direction you may be going. He also uses trials and tribulations in our lives to train us to hear His voice. He may not be big on details, but He is determined to get you through the process. If you are willing to step into the unknown, God is willing to do the impossible.

BE ENCOURAGED!!!

"You posted this at exactly the right time...needed this today more than I can say! Thank you and Bless you Mike...you are the man!" ~ Jane B.

PAY ATTENTION TO WHAT IS PROBABLE.

Yet never lose sight of all that is possible. Remember, settling for what is probable is just an excuse to abandon the least of what is possible. Live knowing that there is never any good reason to settle for less than the best of what can be.

BE ENCOURAGED!!!

DO YOU SOMETIMES FIND YOURSELF IN THE WILDERNESS?

A wilderness that reminds you of how thirsty you are. The kind of wilderness that disturbs your peace. My greatest fear is to exist without living. Fear is our enemy. We fear not accomplishing, but if we don't step out of our comfort zone, we will remain in our wilderness. Devote yourself to an idea. Go make it happen. Struggle in it. Overcome your fears, and don't forget to live life on purpose.

BE ENCOURAGED!!!

IT IS NO ACCIDENT THAT YOU CAME INTO THIS WORLD HEAD FIRST.

Everything starts in your head. Whatever is going on in your head becomes your reality. Using the apple as an example, you can change the peeling, but until you change the core there will not be real change. There is no life in the peeling, but there is life in the core. Only put your efforts into things that are central to your core. Don't chase money, chase your purpose. If you find your purpose, you will find your prosperity. Change your perception and it will change your reality.

BE ENCOURAGED!!!

LOVE FADES WHEN CONDITIONS CHANGE.

It's hard to find compassion when it is painful. Some of those closest to us withdraw when they don't see a benefit. We pour ourselves into people, but people don't pour into us. The moment it is not advantageous, they walk away. We have to open our eyes and if we are not being fed properly, push away from the table.

BE ENCOURAGED!!!

WE ALL HAVE BATTLES.

No one escapes a battle. How do you respond to your battle? Sometimes we are attracted to something that we are horrified of. Petrified and attracted at the same time. One person's meat is another person's poison. Feel the fear but get it under control. Stop fighting the symptoms and go to the source.

BE ENCOURAGED!!!

DO YOU HAVE THE URGE TO JUST QUIT?

Some people have quit school, jobs, relationships, dreaming, and even living. It's not about winning; it's about finishing. You shouldn't care how long it takes as long as you finish...cross the finish line. You may not get a trophy, recognized, or appreciated, but it's not about others, it's about you. It's not what they say about you, it's what you say about yourself. Say to yourself, "I don't quit". Every champion, winner, victorious person has had the urge to quit. Don't give up on your dream because you do make a difference.

Defy the urge to quit!

BE ENCOURAGED!!!

"True!" ~ Rachael A.

People who see obstacles as obstacles will drown. You will always go in the direction of your vision. We must see obstacles as opportunities. We have to find our purpose. With purpose, turbulence doesn't upset us. We are living the best days of our lives and missing it because of not having the proper perspective. Sometimes the greatest times of our lives are in the middle of a storm. If you perceive your situation correctly, your life will change.

BE ENCOURAGED!!!

There are four kinds of criticism I want to highlight.

1. Institutional criticism - when you don't fit into the institutionalized thinking of those around you.

2. Positional criticism – when your critics base everything on their position. They are trained to think a certain way.

3. Intimidation criticism - when your success highlights their deficiencies.

4. Associative criticism - when your critics criticize and attack what you represent.

Your critics come because your brilliance exposes their darkness. Your height exposes their depth. Your integrity exposes their wretchedness. Your victory exposes their defeat. Don't allow the criticism to deter you from the mission. Acknowledging your critics gives them power.

BE ENCOURAGED!!!

DO YOU FEEL LIKE YOU ARE STUCK IN BETWEEN PLACES?

You need to get the strength to birth again and build again. You need to get a new dream, vision, or fire based on the good and bad that has happened in your life. You have been incubated by adversity and have been growing in your groaning. The gulf between need and opportunity can be bridged when you follow your instincts. What do you think about all day and night?

Get up and go after it!!!

BE ENCOURAGED!!!

"This is where I am right now. Thanks, Michael." ~ Angela M.

THE ENEMY KNEW WHO YOU WERE GOING TO BE BEFORE YOU GOT HERE.

He did some things early in the game to mess you up so you couldn't be who God prepared you to be. We are under attack for a reason. Stop taking it personally. The enemy is not after you, he is after your territory, your influence. What do you have that the enemy knew you had early enough to start a storm before you reached your territory? Look back over your life. Things have happened to you because the enemy had more faith in you than you had in yourself. He saw what you would become and it scared him so much he tried to stop you.

BE ENCOURAGED!!!

PEOPLE WANT TO INCARCERATE YOU ON HOW THEY UNDERSTAND YOU TO BE.

What are people saying about you that is stopping you? Will you be limited to how other people define you? We have this inner battle between ordinary and exceptional. Exceptional people refuse to be incarcerated by the parameters of their peers. Exceptional people are not defined by their environment. Being exceptional is the birthing place of creativity. Will you be ordinary or step out and be exceptional? Go to a mirror, look yourself right in the eyes and say,

"I Am Exceptional. "

BE ENCOURAGED!!!

THERE IS NOTHING MORE POWERFUL THAN A CHANGED MIND.

The battle ground between success and struggle, right and wrong, and destiny and failure starts in the mind. You have to change your default settings and have a new normal. If you can't change it in your mind, you can't change it in your life.

BE ENCOURAGED!!!

"Love it love it love it!!" ~ Addie B.

SOMETIMES, SOMEBODY ELSE'S SUCCESS EXACERBATES YOUR OWN FRUSTRATION.

Seeing someone else's accomplishments reminds you that you haven't done as much as you should have to achieve your goals. Feeling this way should nudge you out of your comfort zone and make you not satisfied with where you are. We get to one level of our lives and are so afraid nothing else is going to happen that we settle. You have to sense that you are a person of destiny. Your choices are significant, and what you do matters.

BE ENCOURAGED!!!

YOUR LIFE IS A DIRECT REFLECTION OF THE VOICES YOU LISTEN TO.

Be careful who you surround yourself with because they influence you. How much time have you wasted listening to the wrong voices? People by nature are manipulators. What happens when your life is the end result of others' influences and manipulations? What we should want and need is wisdom, and insight. We do this by allowing the right people to be in our lives.

BE ENCOURAGED!!!

GOD IS A LOVER AND GIVING IS FOR LOVER'S ONLY.

What environment has God designed for you, yet you are not living in? Give yourself permission to receive what God is trying to bring into your life.

BE ENCOURAGED!!!

ARE YOU PUTTING A DEMAND ON LIFE, OR IS LIFE PUTTING A DEMAND ON YOU?

So many of us have lost our appetites for life. We should refuse to just exist. Make things happen rather than have things happen to you. Wake everyday with an agenda, expectations, strategies, and a plan.

BE ENCOURAGED!!!

A PROPER OUTLOOK ON LIFE IS NECESSARY TO CHANGE OUR LIVES.

We must be honest about our environment if we want our outlook on life to change. Your current condition is being fed by your environment. We have to get a new and proper perspective. Your environment is contributing to your disparity. Take a look around; some places we cannot stay. Are you ready to change your perspective? Your outlook is a reflection of what is going on inside you. I'm not where I want to be, but thank God I'm not where I used to be.

BE ENCOURAGED!!!

There is something there that you could say you received amazing Grace in. What you endured was unexplainable, incomprehensible, and mind blowing. It is amazing that someone like you would be doing what you do today. Let's have a funeral today. The old man or woman in you is dead. Let's kill who we used to be so we can become who we are supposed to be.

BE ENCOURAGED!!!

"This is so very appropriate. Was in the hospital for six weeks over the winter due to some mistakes made on my behalf. I got to a point where doctors told my family to start making final arrangements. I know I was supposed to die on March 30th until God showed up in my room. I had my funeral for the old me and decided to move on with the new me. It has done wonders for me. I beat it all and I'm recovering nicely. Let the old you go." ~ Angela

LIVING WITH UNCERTAINTY IS VERY HARD.

You must learn to just say "I don't know". So many of us are afraid of I don't know because 'I know' is our idol. Saying you know makes you look good in front of people, worshipping at the shrine of your own opinion. Experience brings us humility. God has a plan for all of us, but it can't work when we have something else in mind. We find God's glory in the middle of uncertainty. It will come to you when you step out of the way and just say, 'I don't know'. We know our beginning and we know our end, but God knows the middle.

God has made provision in our confusion.

BE ENCOURAGED!!!

Before you start to build your life, you have to be up for the task. There first comes a design and then there is reality. There are no shortcuts to excellence. There is power in the process. People that don't understand the process want the promise without the preparation. Doers do the preparation for the promise. During our preparation, our strength and tolerance increase. Our ability to handle pain increases. Our wisdom increases. Our ability to deal with haters increases. The underground work must be done before aboveground exposure.

BE ENCOURAGED!!!

IF WE STAY AWARE, WE WILL REALIZE THAT GOD ILLUMINATES OUR STEPS.

God knows how to show us the 'what'. We must learn not to fall in love with the gift rather than the giver. We know how to move our physical bodies, but we must learn to move our spirits. The secret place is in the spirit of God. God is our refuge, fortress, and place of protection. God will make a way. We trust him and He will take us to our secret place.

In Him, I will trust.

BE ENCOURAGED!!!

IF YOU LOOK AT THIS WORLD THROUGH THE EYES OF LOGIC, YOU WILL GO CRAZY.

Don't be afraid to be humble. If you have the grace to humble yourself, in due time, you will be exalted. Hold onto your integrity because every moment you suffered is going to come back to you.

BE ENCOURAGED!!!

OUR DESIRES HAVE TO BE PURGED IN THE FIRE OF PRAYER.

We have to figure out if our desire is a Godly desire or a Fleshly desire. We receive our answer in the Spirit before we receive it in our lives. You cannot have it in the Natural unto you receive it in the Spirit. Faith is the substance of things hoped for, evidence of things not seen. We can't imagine the things God has for those that Love him.

BE ENCOURAGED!!!

THERE ARE SOME MIRACLES THAT REQUIRE HUMAN INVOLVEMENT TO GET THEM STARTED.

Get things in order and prepare for your miracle. You have to be prepared so the miracle can continue. So many people are in love with results rather than creating new opportunities. It's called sweat equity. You have to do something that you never did to get something you never had before.

BE ENCOURAGED!!!

DON'T TAKE THE PRESENCE OF THE STORM TO INDICATE THE ABSENCE OF GOD.

Understand that God lives in trouble; He lives in our storms.
As the storm dismantles your boat, do not preserve the
temporary. We put all of our energy into something God only
gave you for a season. Some blessings are not meant to last
the entire journey. You may feel broken but it doesn't mean
you cannot survive. You can make it on broken pieces.
Rough times in life are not in the beginning of a struggle. Be
careful that as you approach the shore you don't drown in
shallow water.

BE ENCOURAGED!!!

YOU HAVE TO GET OUT OF YOUR COMFORT ZONE.

Things are a little hectic now because you are in transition. All the storms and challenges you've gone through are pushing you towards your destiny. Look at the things you've encountered over the last 6 to 12 months. It was all in preparation for where you are going. There were times you thought you wouldn't make it, but you did. You have to change your thinking, rearrange your priorities, and get yourself into alignment. What is before you is greater than what's behind you. Your faith has escaped your past.

BE ENCOURAGED!!!

"Wow, this describes my last 6-12 months so well, especially yesterdays' events for me." ~ Michelle C.

IT'S HARD TO BE BIG WHEN LITTLE HAS YOU.

Little people major in the minor, and minor in the major. Little thinking is entertaining, but not revolutionary. Little thinking will make you stubborn and angry. Little thinking will make you so intent on winning the battle that you lose the war. Stop being little before you miss big opportunities.

BE ENCOURAGED!!!

"Thanks for this post. I am going to copy and post it on my office wall." ~ George C.

"OMG I had to read this twice." ~ Addie B.

YOU ATTRACT THE ENERGY YOU EXUDE.

I thought personality was given to everyone, but I've come to realize that personality is a gift. Pay attention to whom your energy increases and decreases around, because that's the universe giving you a hint of who you should embrace or stray from.

BE ENCOURAGED!!!

BE HONEST WITH LIFE, BE HONEST WITH OTHERS AND, MOST OF ALL BE HONEST WITH YOURSELF.

It is an unwavering commitment to truth and openness that enables you to connect to the power of purpose. May I live and serve the purpose that is within my heart, so that I live my life not for myself, but for those who need me.

BE ENCOURAGED!!!

EXCEPTIONALISM IS OFTEN INCUBATED IN THE WOMB OF ADVERSITY.

Great leaders often come from bad times. Their passion is birthed in the middle of their pain. The more you go through, the more you grow. Stop being satisfied with where you are and strive to reach the next dimension.

BE ENCOURAGED!!!

PEACE IS YOURS TO CHOOSE REGARDLESS OF WHAT ELSE MAY BE GOING ON IN YOUR LIFE.

It will take intention, commitment, and strength, but it is well worth whatever you put into it. Stop living your life from the shallow perspective of your ego and dig deeper within. Today, I give peace a safe, secure, treasured place within, and will continue to let it grow.

BE ENCOURAGED!!!

LIFE IS ABOUT A FIGHT AND YOU HAVE TO KEEP FIGHTING.

It's funny how your perception of other people's fight is actually your normal. People see the good in your life, purely based on what you post on social media. What they don't see is the fight that you may really be going through. If you lose a spouse, keep fighting. If you lose a job, keep fighting. If you lose your health, keep fighting. If life seems to be getting out of control, keep fighting. Finish your race because there is a danger in not finishing. You have to live with the infection of not finishing, and it becomes part of who you are. Forget about winning, just finish.

BE ENCOURAGED!!!

THERE IS A DIFFERENCE BETWEEN WORLDLY PEACE AND SPIRITUAL PEACE.

The difference between peace of the world and the peace of the spirit is in what your peace is born from. The peace of the world is based on what is going on around you. Everything has to be going well to have peace. You react to all external stimuli. You cannot think your best thoughts if you are not in a place of peace. You cannot chase your dreams in an atmosphere of chaos and confusion. God wants to give you crazy peace. There has to be a part of you that you don't submit to your circumstances and situations that you keep protected. This is your secret place. God will meet you in your secret place; the garden of a calm spirit, not moving to the pace the world dictates. Boats don't drown when they are in water, they drown when water gets inside them.

BE ENCOURAGED!!!

WE HAVE TO LEARN TO TRUST GOD WHEN HE SAYS NO.

He says no because His Grace is sufficient. He considered the weight of the load before He put the pain into your life. He knows that you can handle it. Seasoned Saints know how to be overjoyed in tribulation because God is going to show up in your life like He never did before. He is going to increase your weight load, strength, blessings, and your Power. You will have more Integrity, and Divine Power. God trusted you with trouble because you have passed enough tests to show you could Handle it.

BE ENCOURAGED!!!

THE REAL OF TODAY IS IN THE LIVING OF IT.

Be thankful that this day is yours. Express gratitude by thanking God, and then making full use of it. Today is a priceless gift, wanting to be opened. By all means, open it and live its full promise.

BE ENCOURAGED!!!

REAL TROUBLE IS A HUMBLING EXPERIENCE.

You can't help where you have been, but you have control of where you are going. I want you to take pictures of some of the things you are suffering from now so that you can look back and see what you were able to overcome. Bring your life into order and stop the chaos. Empower yourself, get rid of the defeated mentality and break the cycle of bad endings.

BE ENCOURAGED!!!

"You always are inspirational but I love the picture idea."
~ Jane B.

"Thank you for all you do. God's blessings for continued inspiration to push forward. Everyone's journey is unique, your contributions of positivity leak into great beginnings."
~ Ketti G.

YOU ARE A LIVING LETTER FOR ALL TO READ.

Your life is a message visible to all those around you.

What message are you projecting?

BE ENCOURAGED!!!

THINGS GENERALLY DON'T WORK THEMSELVES OUT, YOU HAVE TO WORK THEM OUT YOURSELF.

You need to have the proper perspective and see storms as opportunities. People who see storms as storms, drown because they go in the direction of their vision. People who see storms as opportunities, thrive, and excel. Don't waste your time putting effort and energy into things that are not escalating your destiny. Whatever you put your attention towards, you give life to. Get your face out of the rearview mirror and start looking forward in the direction you are going.

BE ENCOURAGED!!!

THERE IS A DIFFERENCE BETWEEN BEING BURIED AND BEING PLANTED.

Being planted is destiny concealed. Increase is destiny revealed. Between concealed and revealed is called watering. Sometimes we are watered by others, and then there are times we water ourselves. We cry and think our tears are in vain, but God uses our tears to water our dreams. Just because I was planted in a dark place doesn't mean I'm going to stay there.

BE ENCOURAGED!!!

YOU CAN BRING GOOD THINGS OUT OF BAD PLACES.

Bad things happen to good people. We can't allow our situation to keep us captive. There is no captivity worse than a warrior laid up in a bed of worry. Warriors are made for battles, not beds. Faith and fear can cohabitate under the same tent.

Don't let the pain deter you from the purpose.

BE ENCOURAGED!!!

WE ALL HAVE OUR OWN PERSONAL NEST.

We see the world from what we learn in our nest. If you stay in your nest too long, it becomes a curse. Like the eagle stirring her nest, life tends to do the same. When the baby eagles return to the nest after it is stirred, they find that it is uncomfortable. We go through seasons of discomfort. Your potential is too big for your nest. What was once your protector, now is your prison. Don't die in your nest.

BE ENCOURAGED!!!

DON'T LET WHERE YOU START DEFINE WHERE YOU ARE GOING.

It's not about the destination; it's about the journey. There is a direct connection between progress and struggle. The more external pressure you encounter, the more internal strength you gain. The more challenges you have, the more you grow. Remember, even when it doesn't look good, it's all good.

BE ENCOURAGED!!!

LIFE HAS A TENDENCY TO TEACH US LESSONS.

I'm learning that the word Service means nothing to many in this world. You cannot be accomplished without the ultimate sacrifice of self. There are many people who are takers and not givers. They are only interested if they are getting fed. Sacrificing yourself for others brings great peace and satisfaction.

BE ENCOURAGED!!!

DON'T LET THE NEGATIVE WORDS SPOKEN OVER YOUR LIFE DETERMINE WHO YOU BECOME.

The words that others speak get deep down inside you, and you become pregnant with them. Words are seeds and they germinate in your heart. If you don't abort these seeds, you will become what they say. You have to be transformed by the renewing of your mind.

BE ENCOURAGED!!!

"Perfect for those in my business. My new adventure."
~ Angela M.

THERE IS NO HAPPINESS IN POVERTY AND NO HAPPINESS IN THE PALACE.

If you are in poverty, don't envy the palace. Sometimes the oxymoron of life is that being in the palace can be just as sad as poverty. Be careful not to allow your imagination of perfection to override reality. Haters hate because they hate to see you celebrate while they suffer. Understand what matters.

BE ENCOURAGED!!!

IT'S NOT THE SUCCESS THAT SHOWS WHO YOU REALLY ARE.

Your strength is perfected in the weak times of life; how you handle the hurts of life. I call them good hurts because they made me tougher, better and stronger. The good hurts killed the boy in me so the man in me could be released.

BE ENCOURAGED!!!

FAITHFUL ARE THE WORDS OF A FRIEND.

We need friends who will tell us the truth even if it may hurt us. You see a real friend is an investment, so surround yourself with those who are willing to invest the time. The kisses of an enemy are deceitful. Be careful of those who kiss you and hate you at the same time. We must have a degree of discernment and surround ourselves with those who are about our best interest.

BE ENCOURAGED!!!

THE MIND IS A POWERFUL, COMPLICATED, SOPHISTICATED MACHINE.

If you want new beginnings, you have to have a renewed mind. Without a renewed mind, you will only repeat the old cycle. You have to move somethings out of the way because you cannot build your future in the dark. Things that affect your vision can affect your destiny. You have to get rid of stinking thinking, and embrace new thoughts, plan, attitude, and vision.

BE ENCOURAGED!!!

DO YOU HAVE THE INSTINCT TO INCREASE IN YOUR LIFE?

First of all, don't waste your time with comparing yourself to others. When you compare yourself to others, jealousy is born and you cannot be jealous and creative at the same time. There is nothing more valuable than an opportunity. Opportunities will come dressed up as opposition. Truly accomplished people are afraid, but the difference is they feel the fear, but override it. It's what you do with the fear. You can make it excellence or excuses.

BE ENCOURAGED!!!

STOP RUNNING.

When you run from one thing, you will run from everything. Stop running and face what you fear. You will not be the greatest you if you continue to run from things that scare you. You have to fall in love with yourself in the process. Don't limit your perception of what you can truly be. You can't conquer what you don't confront.

BE ENCOURAGED!!!

"Just the reminder I needed right now!!!" ~ Rachael A.

HOW CAN SOMETHING BE IN THE WILL OF GOD AND STILL GO WRONG?

Even when things went wrong they were actually right. All things work together for the good of those who love God. Things may not work for what you want, but they work for what God wants. He sets it up and then sets it off. What has hurt you becomes the wind that blows you into your destiny. Believing in this will drive regret totally out of your life.

BE ENCOURAGED!!!

INFORMATION MEANS NOTHING WITHOUT REVELATION.

We are not bound to where we have been. We could be fed information all day, but until you have a revelation, you will not see it. Revelation shines a light on information so you can use it. You cannot deal with what you don't understand. Isolation is really a reservation. You have to go through a period of uncertainty and isolation to realize it's all a set up for a divine revelation.

BE ENCOURAGED!!!

THE POTHOLES IN YOUR LIFE DON'T COME WITH ANNOUNCEMENTS OR ROAD SIGNS.

Nothing can prepare you for the unexpected potholes as you move towards your destiny. You hit some smaller potholes and there is little damage, but there are some potholes that make you pull over. It makes you check and see how much damage you may be carrying after the pothole. The potholes are planned to separate the functional from the dysfunction in your life. It kills the things that need to die so other things can be born. Potholes don't mean you are not going to reach your destiny. You are just delayed, not denied.

BE ENCOURAGED!!!

"Thanks. I need this today." ~ Wendy S.

LIGHT ALWAYS CASTS A SHADOW.

Stop trying to figure out why they don't like you. You did nothing; your light just got too bright.

When someone else's significance is diminished by your presence, they become a secret enemy.

BE ENCOURAGED!!!

THE PERFECT GIFT IS FROM ABOVE.

God planted it down inside us. Tragedy is squandering the gift He has planted. We must use our gift for gain. Some of us are blessed with million-dollar gifts and are using them in welfare situations. Remember, the greater the gift, the greater the responsibility. You have to give back to what has been given to you. The difference between a robber and a customer is the customer pays for their items where the robber just takes.

BE ENCOURAGED!!!

WHAT IS THE DESTINY THAT GOD HAS FOR YOU?

You were created with a specific purpose in mind. God has predestined your life. He has planned your beginning and end. Be careful not to waste your time going after things that are not yours. Some of you think you have reached your destination, but you are actually only at your rehearsal.

BE ENCOURAGED!!!

LIFE IS A SERIES OF BEING DRAWN OUT.

In between every system of sustenance there will be sorrow.
You will always go from lesser to larger. You will be growing
in your groaning, but you will have the victory.

BE ENCOURAGED!!!

WHEN YOU HAVE A STRATEGY THAT ALIGNS WITH YOUR PURPOSE YOU DON'T NEED MUCH TO MAKE IT WORK.

When your strategy is undergirded by a sense of divine purpose, God will take less and do more. If you look at your life in pieces, you will make bad choices. Looking at the pieces blocks your understanding of the good and bad that happens in your life. Don't define yourself by one phase in your life. Everything that happens in your life is strategic.

BE ENCOURAGED!!!

THE PRINCIPLE OF SOWING AND REAPING IS NOT MAGIC.

You have to be able to see the value coming back to you in your life. The conflict is in the integrity of the seed which is in you. You have to get your core values in order. The enemy comes to devalue the seed. Just look at the things that have been planted in your life to devalue you. The enemy tries to rob the seed of the nutrients that fuel you. The greater the attack the greater the value.

BE ENCOURAGED!!!

FEAR IS POWERFUL, AND YET FRAGILE.

Though it can stop you cold, fear can be gone in an instant when you decide you've had enough of it. By letting go of fear, you transform it into courage, and you put the power of that fear into positive use. Boldly step through each fear, move past it, and feel the strength that is gained.

BE ENCOURAGED!!!

EXPERIENCES VERSUS OUR INSTINCTS IS WHAT KEEPS US IN OUR CAGE.

Experiences form your intellect which becomes your background. Your instinct senses something that you have yet to touch. Being safe is not satisfying. The familiar doesn't mean it's right. Experiences contradict our instincts. Don't be afraid of where you have come from. Our past may create a limp, but the limp is a reminder of how much freedom cost. Get over this next hurdle and the sun will be shining on your face.

BE ENCOURAGED!!!

YOUR MIND IS YOUR POWER.

If I was your enemy, the first thing that I would attack is your mind. When your mind is under attack, you lose your creativity, passion, and your sense of being an influence. The enemy is after your mind, using what you care about most to drive you crazy. Don't be so distracted by what could happen tomorrow that you miss the pleasures of today. Some of us are living our lives out of focus. We need detail so we don't make dumb decisions. Your mind is your power and your power is in your mind.

BE ENCOURAGED!!!

WE MUST HAVE THE INSTINCT TO SHIFT GEARS.

Many of us are stuck in first gear. The God I serve is a strategic God. He's intelligent, articulate, and profound. He expects us to change the world by using whatever we have been through to drive us. Success is a science not an art.

BE ENCOURAGED!!!

What is unique about you?
What drives you?
What disturbs you?
What do you disturb?

Good people go through bad things because when God gets ready to unlock what's in you, He will always do it in a dark place. You can't branch out until you reach in. Remember intellect loads the gun but instinct pulls the trigger.

BE ENCOURAGED!!!

DON'T BE A DREAMER OR A WANNABE.

Where you are isn't as important as where you are going. Stop having stinking thinking, negative attitudes, and low self-worth. Frustration is rooted in what you think about yourself. Be a person of action. When you see it, go after it. When you get it, don't wait for others to celebrate you. Throw your own party and celebrate yourself.

BE ENCOURAGED!!!

LISTEN, YOUR INSTINCTS MAY BE TELLING YOU THAT THIS COULD BE A DESTINY MOMENT.

Sit for a moment, quiet yourself and listen to your spirit. The answers you've been looking for are inside of you. You just have to follow your instincts. When you feel that passion line up with that pain, go after it because you have a destiny to fulfill.

BE ENCOURAGED!!!

GOD'S ANSWERS DON'T ALWAYS LOOK LIKE WHAT WE HAVE IN MIND.

Miracles are made out of need. If there is not a need to challenge you, there will not be a word to stir you. God will bless you in your famine, but the drought around you will continue. God does the greatest things with just a little bit. Your cup may not run over, but each time you reach back God provides for you.

BE ENCOURAGED!!!

FAILURE IS ASSOCIATED WITH THE FEELING THAT YOU ARE ALMOST THERE.

When you experience abnormal failure, there is a spiritual principle being illustrated. When God closes a door, it's permanently closed. You have to figure out that God is *the* way not *a* way. The God of the questions is the God of the answers. When you experience your greatest failure, you are closest to your greatest victory.

BE ENCOURAGED!!!

THE WORLD WORKS IN SYSTEMS OF CYCLES.

You must feed what is feeding you. Give to what is giving to you. Bless what is blessing you. Help who is helping you. You must pour into what is pouring into you. Any relationship that violates reciprocity is cursed. You must give to what is giving to you and if not, it will kill the source. You cannot be disrespectful and expect honor. You cannot be greedy and expect prosperity. You cannot be hostile and expect love. Ask yourself the question...

What area of your life are you under funding and over expecting?

BE ENCOURAGED!!!

WE ALL HAVE SURVIVED SOMETHING AND HAVE HAD THE URGE TO QUIT.

It's dangerous to give up. You cannot be a champion until you survive a breaking point. Don't let the cares of this world destroy your passion for living. You have to run after your destiny. Success is never an accident, success is intentional. When you run after your destiny, you distance yourself from your history. Wash your past off or you will forfeit moving forward.

BE ENCOURAGED!!!

SOMETIMES WE ARE IN A WILDERNESS WHERE NOTHING GROWS.

A wilderness that reminds us of how thirsty we are. A wilderness that disturbs our rest. Always remember that the barking of the haters should remind you of the promise to come. Many people live and die in the wilderness of uncertainty. Some people live and die not knowing who they are. Please don't settle for mediocrity and less than God's purpose for you. Don't settle for mediocrity instead of greatness. Profit is determined not by how you fight, how you stood, how many victories you've had. Profit is what you have left once the transaction is completed.

BE ENCOURAGED!!!

WE ARE RUNNING OUT OF TIME.

What are you going to do with the time you have left? You have to reposition yourself or you can miss the best time of your life. Change the way you think, function, and deal with life issues. Some of us are stuck between the lines of limited thinking and limited people. You must have courage to take risk and expand your mind to a new level of thinking. What is hiding in you that you don't see? What strength are you under-utilizing? This is your moment and you must be determined to live it. The best is yet to come.

BE ENCOURAGED!!!

"Woo hoo!! Let's find our best. Read this every day."
~ Addie B.

IF YOU WANT TO WIN THE BATTLE OF LIFE, YOU HAVE TO STAY ON TRACK.

Be careful of discouragement because it can hide in your life. It can even hide behind a smile. Be careful not to make permanent decisions in a temporary circumstance. Life involves steps and steps imply progress; it will take a while. Remember that Blessings too soon are not Blessings at all. My Agony makes my Ecstasy. My Sickness makes my Healing. My Poverty makes my Prosperity.

The value of a man is based on his ability to press on.

BE ENCOURAGED!!!

Faith is a verb. You have to do something. Faith does not demand details. Faith only works if you do something. Faith only works if you work it. You are not waiting on God, God is waiting on you. Stand on the promises of God and watch him move supernaturally in your life.

BE ENCOURAGED!!!

A LESSON IN HUMILITY.

How would life really be if people were genuinely humble, completely selfless and putting others before themselves? You can be humble without low self-esteem. You have to be strong to be humble. You have to be secure and have an understanding of yourself so you don't need validation from others. Know who you are, have a sense of purpose and serve others. It's a creed that I live by.

BE ENCOURAGED!!!

YOU HAVE TO WORK WITH THE SKIN THAT YOU WERE BORN WITH.

Be happy with it or you will never be happy. You are only effective when you are your most authentic self. So many people want promotion without process. You have to be patient with the process, and not enthralled with the promise. Stop being busy trying to make progress and neglect where you are. Stop being in love with tomorrow and neglecting today.

BE ENCOURAGED!!!

"Thanks for the words of wisdom and encouragement."
~ Leopold G.

So many people have endured some bad times. They are not moving on. They are stuck, just enjoying the fact that they survived, bringing down their expectations to match their reality. You have to surround yourself with people who want more out of life than just surviving. You cannot hang out with blind people and expect to see. Stop being addicted to your infliction. Success is intentional so run after your destiny.

BE ENCOURAGED!!!

GOD GIVES YOU TRIALS TO PREPARE YOU FOR WHAT IS COMING NEXT.

Your trials are preparation for the next challenge and there is nothing better than experience. You need to throw your history at your destiny. You have to sometimes go backwards to go forwards. Go back to your foundation to see what makes you tick. What is your story? Your blessings are always in your battles. Your greatness is delivered in your weakness. Until you learn to humble yourself, you will never kill your giant. Serve others with excellence and you will make a name for yourself.

BE ENCOURAGED!!!

"Thank you for your post! Need this." ~ Arnice V.

EXCEPTIONAL AND ORDINARY ALWAYS HAVE A CONFLICT.

Anytime exceptional people hang out around ordinary people, there is going to be conflict. So, if you are exceptional, limit your time with ordinary people. I refuse to live up to dead interpretations of my life. I'm a trend setter, a rule breaker, an exceptional human being.

BE ENCOURAGED!!!

BE ENCOURAGED!!!

Connect with me at:

www.michaelarterberry.com

https://www.facebook.com/michael.arterberry

https://www.linkedin.com/in/michaelarterberry/